An Asperger's Guide to Public Speaking

Parts of Chapters 4 and 14 have been adapted from *An Asperger's Guide to Entrepreneurship: Setting Up Your Own Business for Leader with Autism Spectum Disorder*, published by Jessica Kingsley Publishers 2014.

First published in 2015
by Jessica Kingsley Publishers
73 Collier Street
London N1 9BE, UK
and
400 Market Street, Suite 400
Philadelphia, PA 19106, USA

www.jkp.com

Library of Congress Cataloging in Publication Data
A CIP catalog record for this book is available from the Library of Congress

British Library Cataloguing in Publication Data
A CIP catalogue record for this book is available from the British Library

ISBN 978 1 84905 516 1
eISBN 978 0 85700 979 1

This book is dedicated to all those outstanding individuals
I have had the privilege to work with, mentor and support.
I hope you know that you inspire me as much as I hope I inspire you.

Acknowledgements

Acknowledgements are initially due to all the remarkable fellow Aspergerians I have had the privilege of liaising with as a result of my work with Asperger Leaders. I would additionally like to extend my thanks to my editorial team at Jessica Kingsley Publishers, in particular Emily McClave and Sarah Minty, for sharing my vision for a series of business development books for people on the spectrum.

Contents

Introduction

Over the last decade there has been more and more awareness of autism and Asperger syndrome, together with the realisation that there are a lot of people on the autistic spectrum holding senior roles within business. However, there is still a marked stereotype in respect of what a person with high-functioning autism or Asperger syndrome is and is not capable of doing in the corporate world – a stereotype that sees this individual as solitary, technically-minded, possibly quasi-compulsive in their activities and difficult to work with.

In reality, there are a number of very successful business leaders in the corporate world who have Asperger syndrome or high-functioning autism. I count myself as one of them. Far from being introverted technology geeks, we are strong business leaders and visionaries. Where appropriate, we have successfully learned to cope with the additional challenges we may have encountered as a result of our developmental disorder, as well as optimising the unique skills and advantages this condition offers us. This achievement is something that should be recognised and celebrated, yet frequently many of us feel the need to hide our diagnosis because of the stigma associated with the term 'autism' and the threat (be it direct or indirect) this may represent for our continued career progression.

There are often a number of areas of performance where Asperger leaders may feel disadvantaged compared to the average neurotypical in the workplace, either due to the genuine differences in the way our brains process information, or due to our own – frequently incorrect – concern that we are just not as good in certain areas as neurotypicals. As a business leader with Asperger syndrome, I include myself in this observation, and it took me a number of years as a business leader to recognise areas where I could develop alternative coping strategies to neurotypicals, areas where I did not actually need to develop any coping strategies, and even areas where I actually performed far better than the average neurotypical purely due to the unique working of the autistic brain.

The purpose of this book is to share with other people on the autistic spectrum some of the insights I have developed over the years in respect to one of the areas of business that many people on the spectrum feel can be particularly challenging – public speaking. Contrary to what the stereotypical perception of people with Asperger's dictates, I believe that we actually have a very strong proclivity towards speaking about topics of special interest to us, and that this inclination can be successfully channelled towards developing a strong public speaking voice in any area of business, be it an area of particular interest or not. What is important to recognise is that the effects of public speaking for someone with Asperger's does not start when the person steps up to the podium and end when they step down. For us, there is more to prepare for, deal with and follow through on as a direct consequence of our Asperger syndrome. Hence, while there are many exceptionally good books on public speaking per se, it is the additional areas that I will be speaking about that make this book unique and useful for people on the spectrum than any general book on public speaking.

The examples and case studies in this book are taken from the experiences of people who have found themselves in situations that are possibly similar to your own, and the book itself is written by someone who has been there herself. While my predominant focus is to assist business leaders and professionals at all career levels who are on the autistic spectrum to prepare for public speaking on behalf of their organisations, the tools and techniques I have included here will be useful for anyone on the autistic spectrum who wants to undertake public speaking activities. I encourage you make use of the tools and exercises in this book to assist you in your career development by including the necessary – and exciting – area of public speaking. Part 5 contains a number of toolkits and exercises which are available to be downloaded from www.jkp.com/uk/an-asperger-s-guide-to-public-speaking.html.

Before I continue, a note about terminology. Many of us have been diagnosed as having Asperger syndrome. This name has its origin from the person who first recognised and wrote about the syndrome, Hans Asperger, in the 1940s. Asperger's work was not of particular interest at the time, but there was a resurgence of interest in his work in the 1980s, and the term Asperger syndrome (or Asperger's disorder) was named after him posthumously, only in 1994 being officially recognised in the Diagnostic and Statistical Manual of Mental Disorders (DSM), published by the American Psychiatric Association, 2013.

The DSM was created to enable mental health professionals to communicate using a common diagnostic language and standard criteria for the classification of mental disorders. It was first published in 1952, but because our understanding of mental health is evolving, the DSM is periodically updated. In each revision, mental health conditions that are no longer considered valid are removed, while newly defined conditions are added. In 2013, the fifth edition of DSM was issued.

One of the most important changes in the fifth edition of the Diagnostic and Statistical Manual of Mental Disorders (DSM-V) is from Asperger syndrome to autism spectrum disorder (ASD). The revised diagnosis represents a new, more accurate, and medically and scientifically useful way of diagnosing individuals with autism-related disorders.

Using DSM-IV, patients could be diagnosed with four separate disorders: autistic disorder, Asperger's disorder, childhood disintegrative disorder, or the catch-all diagnosis of pervasive developmental disorder not otherwise specified. Researchers found that these separate diagnoses were not consistently applied across different clinics and treatment centres. Anyone diagnosed with one of the four pervasive developmental disorders (PDD) from DSM-IV should still meet the criteria for ASD in DSM-V or another, more accurate DSM-V diagnosis. While DSM does not outline recommended treatment and services for mental disorders, determining an accurate diagnosis is a first step for a clinician in defining a treatment plan for a patient.

In line with the above changes, this book is intended to apply to all people who fall within the category of Autism Spectrum Disorder (ASD), as defined in the DSM-V, including those of us who have previously been diagnosed as having Asperger syndrome. This in no way detracts from our unique contributions as Asperger leaders, but seeks to ensure that anyone being diagnosed under the new, all-inclusive classification realises that this book applies to them too.

Chapter 1

I Don't Need to Speak Publicly Right Now, So Why Worry About It?

For most of us with an autistic spectrum disorder working in the business world, public speaking is certainly not something that we tend to focus on as a core part of our role. While we may recognise that at some stage in the future it is likely that we will be required to speak on behalf of the company, many of us feel that we are adequately prepared to do this and therefore do not really think about it until such time as the need arises. So why should we actually spend time focusing on how we handle public speaking if the requirement for us to do so is not imminent?

Or you could be someone who has already made your career step into a leadership role in your company and are focusing on the more strategic outlook of your work. As a leader in your area, it is up to you to decide how you spend your time. So why should you be worrying about public speaking if this isn't something you want to do or are currently that interested in doing? Many people who move into leadership roles in business are lulled into a false sense of security about the need to speak publicly. Many feel that they will never have to address the issue, since now that they are in their leadership role, they can always decline any requests for public speaking. But is this really the case?

Let me suggest a few situations that may arise now or in your career in the future where you may very well be faced with the requirement to speak publicly with little or no warning beforehand.

Press interviews/media meetings

Sometimes events can happen within your organisation that require a press or media conference at short notice. While many people rely on the fact that the organisation may have a public relations or communication person, in the event of a particularly important or newsworthy occurrence, it is may be expected of you to be the person addressing the media. Given this situation, would you know how to present yourself and adequately represent your company?

Holding staff meetings or presenting at internal meetings at short notice

Often it is necessary for senior managers within business to hold all staff (or all division) meetings. These are generally done in the form of a formal speech or presentation. If you were asked to do this at short notice, would you know how to present yourself to your staff in such a way that reflected confidence and allowed your staff to trust you? If you were asked to present to your colleagues on a project that you are working on, would you know how to control your nerves and get your message across?

Putting forward a case for investment or funding

If you hold a senior position in business, there could very well be a point where you will be required to seek additional funding for your business. Frequently, this is done by presentations to potential stakeholders or investors. In many cases this is undertaken in the form of a meeting, but occasionally this can take the form of a public speaking event. If you were asked to do this at short notice, do you think you would be able to cope?

Being called to make an impromptu presentation in a meeting

Even if you are relatively new within your chosen career or in the business, situations can arise where you can unexpectedly be asked to speak in front of others. For example, you might attend a quarterly meeting for your global functional area. While this type of meeting would generally be an opportunity for you to learn from more senior members of your function, you may be surprised when your regional manager mentions a specific piece of work you have been doing and asks you to speak to the meeting about it. For many people this could really catch them off guard, since they would not have had time to prepare for a presentation, and will need to rely on speaking to the meeting 'off the cuff'. How you present yourself in this type of situation can have implications for your ongoing career development in the company, and therefore is very important.

Standing in for your manager at a client meeting

As a junior member of a sales or business development team, you will frequently have the opportunity to join your manager at a sales pitch in order to learn how to do this effectively as part of your own personal development. However, there is always the potential that things will change unexpectedly. For example, you could arrived at a client's office to present details of a new product to the client, only to receive a text message from your manager to say that he has been held up. As a result, you need to be the person who presents the details of the product as part of the sales pitch. As per the earlier scenarios, you would not have had an opportunity to prepare for this, and would in all likelihood find it particularly challenging. So how would you deal with it?

The above scenarios are just some examples of the types of event that could result in you being called to speak at short notice. Most people are actually quite unaware of the challenges in undertaking a public speaking event, and this is especially true for those of us on the autistic spectrum.

There are a number of reasons for those of us with an ASD to do some preparatory work on public speaking ahead of any requirement to actually speak publicly, some of which are as relevant for neurotypicals as they are for us. However, there is the potential for us to experience a sensory overload if we do not prepare adequately, or to become otherwise overwhelmed.

It is important to understand that we become successful public speakers not only by reading books or listening to the advice of others, but by actually practising. For this reason, the exercises I have included in this book are particularly important for people on the spectrum who want to become successful public speakers. In general, most people do not always have that much advance notice of the need to speak publicly, especially in the business situation, and therefore it is important for you to start learning and practising sooner rather than later. This will give you the additional time you need to develop and integrate your new skills to be a natural part of your speaking style and preparation, so that when you are asked to speak publicly you know you are ready, and can focus on the preparation of your speech rather than having to prepare yourself for the event as well.

I will cover a number of essential areas of preparation, including personal preparation, dealing with overload issues, identifying and overcoming some of your personal challenges in speaking, and developing and presenting an optimal speech. I will also cover in detail areas that most public speaking books do not, such as the practical issues you need to deal with before you speak, and how to cope with post-speech networking and any overload issues. This will assist you in your preparation for and delivery of your future public speaking engagements.

PART 1

Getting Ready for Public Speaking – Before You Need to Do It

Chapter 2

Defining the Asperger Challenges and Strengths

In the age of information sharing and global communication, a central part of any business executive's role is the ability to share information in a public setting – what we know as public speaking. Unlike in the previous century, public speaking has become far more prevalent due to technological advances which have made presentations, conferences and even web-conferences far more accessible to a global audience. No longer are business executives only expected to speak publicly if they have a particularly high profile. Nowadays there are so many conferences, workshops and presentations that public speakers are actively sought from the business community, and the Boards of Directors or organisations are expecting their leaders and employees at all levels to play an active part in this activity in order to present their organisation to the public.

Individuals with Asperger syndrome or high functioning autism within business are sometimes unprepared for the requirement they face to speak publicly. Although the same can be said for any individual, it is important to recognise that for those of us on the autistic spectrum there may be quite a bit more preparation required to make sure that we are ready to handle this new challenge.

Public speaking for any person on the spectrum can be seen to have similar challenges, whether they are speaking as a business leader or speaking as someone with a specialist interest in a particular subject, as an advocate for some cause or as an academic.

While there can be additional challenges for people on the autistic spectrum when it comes to public speaking, people with ASD generally have a significant advantage over neurotypicals when it comes to speaking about areas of particular interest to them. This can be clarified by looking at what I believe to be the five key areas through which individuals make an impact in their public speaking. These areas are:

- *Self-knowledge* – Having an understanding of your own personal speaking style, areas that make you unique, and a full understanding of and mechanism to apply any necessary coping or adjustment techniques that are all your own.

- *Passion and charisma* – Feeling impassioned about what you are speaking about and being able to captivate your audience and inspire them in some way using this passion.

- *Empathy* – Speaking to an audience and being able to understand and/or perceive how they are reacting to your message.

- *Authority* – Speaking about your topic with confidence and in such a way that the audience trusts you and hence sees you as an expert on the topic.

- *Knowledge* – Having the necessary facts and information covering the topic being discussed, over and above the level of knowledge of the average member of the audience.

These key areas can be remembered by using the acronym SPEAK. As you develop your public speaking skills, be it in the area of preparing your speech, preparing yourself, speaking or networking afterwards, make sure that you keep the five elements of SPEAK in your mind.

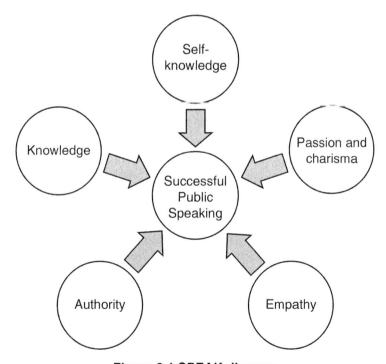

Figure 2.1 SPEAK diagram

I will discuss the above elements of public speaking as we progress through the book. Now I want to consider these from the perspective of our autistic strengths and challenges.

One key advantage those of us on the spectrum have is that when it comes to an area of particular interest of ours, we tend to be the subject matter experts. We are the knowledge sponges, soaking up relevant information and keeping it deep within us. When it is a special interest for us, we will tend to have an incredible amount of information about the topic, just because this tends to be the way our brains work. If there is additional information to be gleaned on a topic of interest, without a doubt we will find it! As a result, the element of *knowledge* tends to be one in which we excel.

Another element where we tend to excel is that of *passion*. No-one can deny that when we speak about something that is of particular interest to us, we tend to be extremely passionate. If it is something that is important to us, it really is important to us! If we are interested in something, we tend to put our whole heart into it, and while passion itself certainly is not a characteristic that is unique to those of us on the spectrum, I would say that it is our level of dedication and focus that makes the difference.

If we now consider the element of *authority*, many people would assume that – given our high levels of knowledge – being perceived as an authority on the topic would be a given. Actually, it is not purely the level of our knowledge that makes people consider us authorities. What is even more important is the confidence with which we present the knowledge we have. This may sound strange, but that is why some people who are far less knowledgeable on a subject can be perceived as greater authorities than those with the actual knowledge. Have you ever attended a conference or speaking event where you have heard someone speaking on a topic and you have felt that the level of their expertise is not actually as high as we would expect it to be for someone claiming to be a specialist, only to hear other people lauding their presentation and knowledge levels? I know I have. At first I used to find this incredibly confusing. How could someone with just generic know-how be seen as more of an expert than the professor with an overwhelming amount of knowledge who had umm-ed and aaah-ed his way through his presentation. The answer lies in just how the knowledge was presented. So presentation skills are critical to your impact and your ongoing reputation in the area in which you are speaking. For those of us on the spectrum, this means that we need to do a bit more preparation, since the ability to consider how we are coming across to an audience is not a skill that comes naturally to us. However, with the right guidance, this is an area we can learn to excel in.

You would expect the element of *empathy* to be the one area where perhaps we would struggle the most. However, I would like to start by saying that this is not necessarily the case. Having empathy means that you are able to identify with the emotions and feelings of the people you are speaking to. While I do agree that – once again – this may be an area that does not come naturally to most of us, if we are speaking about something we are passionate about, we actually can and do empathise with the people we are speaking to. For example, I speak about people on the autistic spectrum and some of the challenges we experience in the workplace. In speaking to other people on the spectrum, I know exactly how they are feeling, what their challenges are likely to be and what emotions they are experiencing – because I have been there. This is a level of insight a neurotypical could never have, no matter how extensive their professional or personal experience.

Another element we may need to focus on as people on the spectrum is *charisma*. I am absolutely not saying that people on the spectrum are not naturally charismatic, because many are. However, what I think is essential to this charisma being successful in a public speaking environment is for you as an individual to see and recognise in exactly what way you are charismatic. We need to ensure that we recognise what is perceived as positive and what is not, and then ensure that our public speaking persona reflects the parts that do work far more powerfully than any that do not. Key to doing this is to ensure we have full *self-knowledge* of our strengths, our weaknesses, our uniqueness and what areas we need to work on or emphasise.

Personal speaking versus speaking on behalf of your company

There is another aspect to the challenge of public speaking. There is a big difference between speaking on a topic for which you have a particular personal interest and undertaking a speaking engagement on behalf of your organisation. You may be surprised to hear me say that – surely public speaking is public speaking? Well – yes and no, I'm afraid. Let me explain.

When you speak about something you have a particularly strong interest in or are passionate about, it goes without saying that you will automatically be a knowledge expert, that you are going to display your passion for the topic, and you are going to engage with the audience because it is likely that they share a similar – if not the same – interest. You will have a wealth of information to share, and if anything you will need to think about when to stop talking because it can be very tempting to go on and on and on!

Let's take now the scenario of you being asked to speak on behalf of your organisation. True, it could still be on a topic that you are particularly interested in, but in all likelihood it is not really going to be a passion of yours. For example, while you may be interested in the success of the organisation, you may not be particularly interested in the financial statements of the business, or particular business activities that the company many want you to focus on in the speaking engagement. Hence, looking at our five key elements of successful speaking:

- *Self-knowledge* – It is important for you to understand and recognise how you react to having to share information on a topic that is not of particular interest to you. Do you speak enthusiastically up to that point, then drop into a monotone? Do you engage your audience up to that point, then suddenly drop your eyes and end up 'reading your notes' during the less interesting part of the speech? Do you start stimming? This all makes up self-knowledge. Once you know if you do adopt any inappropriate practices, you can then develop strategies to ensure that you deal with this optimally.

- *Passion and charisma* – There is nothing stopping us from being passionate about our business presentation, but it frequently is not a very natural response. There certainly are areas of business that will naturally lend themselves to a passionate response (for example, if you are launching a new product that you are really excited about), but often business speaking is not quite so dramatic. What you need to be able to do is develop the ability to get impassioned about any speech, irrespective of the topic, and to be able to project that passion to your audience. As far as charisma is concerned, while may people can understand being charismatic when it comes to a topic of personal interest, they struggle with the idea of coming across as charismatic in a business environment. Again, this is a skill that can be developed so that you reflect your natural charisma in all public speaking events, not just those of personal importance to you.

- *Empathy* – In a business presentation environment the concept of empathy is directly linked to visually identifying where your audience is. By this I mean that you will be required to be far more perceptive in respect of your audience's body language, and this can be difficult for those of us on the spectrum unless we prepare ourselves beforehand with some additional skills.

- *Authority* – You may not feel that you actually are the authority on the topic, and this lack of confidence is likely to be apparent to your audience.

- *Knowledge* – This is closely linked to the previous point. As mentioned, you may or may not be the most knowledgeable person in this respect, or at least you may not feel that you have the levels of knowledge that you would prefer to have. This in itself could make you feel less confident.

I will provide you with some case studies to show you how other people have addressed similar challenges, as well as a number of exercises to help you identify and develop your own public speaking persona later on. There are also some aimed at assisting you in dealing with the very ASD specific issues such as sensory overload, stress management and confidence issues.

As you end this chapter, can I suggest that you take the time to go to Part 5 of the book and complete Toolkit Exercise 1: Your Initial Thoughts (p.148) in preparation for the work you will do throughout the rest of the book.

Chapter 3

Types of Public Speaking

When people think about the concept of public speaking, many consider that this is a single type of event and that any topics of discussion are referring to the same phenomena. In fact, there are a number of different types of public speaking, each of which has its own unique nuances and challenges. If you are to be adequately prepared to speak in public, you need to be aware of what the various types of speaking are and how they differ.

The first type is that where you *speak on behalf of yourself as a specialist or professional*, talking about your particular area of interest. This is the type most people think about first of all when considering public speaking. In fact, many people consider that this is the only type of public speaking. But, as you will see below, there certainly are other types that do not fall into this category. Speaking on behalf of yourself as a specialist or professional is where you speak on your particular topic of interest: your passion; your focus. This can be done at specialist conferences, universities, schools – it depends on what your specialist area is and who your audience would be.

Another type of public speaking where we are able to do equally well is that of *academic speaking*. Academic speaking, as the name implies, is where we speak to academic colleagues, peers or professionals on an academic topic. Generally this is undertaken in venues such as universities, colleges or academic seminar or conferences. I would also include certain types of lecturing under this heading, since in these cases you are making an academic presentation to an audience of students.

After these types of public speaking, we start to move to the very different situation of speaking on behalf of your company. There are a number of levels of company speaking, and it would be fair to say that although the first types I will be describing here are actually more in line with internal presentations than public speaking, I mention them as an indicator of how your speaking will progress as you continue to represent your organisation. The first of these company level speaking arrangements is that of *making a presentation to your internal team*. For those of us who manage people, learning how to interact with your team is a critical skill, one which I will be covering in a separate book. A key aspect is being able to present to your team as a whole in a more formal format. This could be, for example, doing a presentation to them about changes coming up in the company, giving feedback on team performance, introducing a new incentive scheme, and so forth. In general, speaking to your internal team is often considered more of a management challenge than a public speaking one. However, the same principles of how you present yourself and your message apply when you are speaking to your staff as they would if you were speaking to an external audience. Your team is your audience.

The next level of presentation up from presenting to your internal team is *presenting internally to your company*. In this situation, you are making a speech or presentation to the company as a whole (or a broader part of it) rather than just your team. Examples of this type of speaking include speaking to the company at the annual business celebration event, or speaking to the organisation to announce that you are going to be merging with another organisation. While many of the people you will be speaking to here are still individuals you work with, by far the largest proportion will actually be people employed by your company but not working with or reporting directly to you. Once again, this can be very challenging for some people unless they have taken the time to prepare themselves beforehand.

Continuing up the ladder of business speaking, we then reach the activity *speaking on behalf of your company at a public event*. Here you will have been asked to represent your company at an external event, speaking on a subject determined by or agreed with your leadership team. Examples of this would be where you attend a 'green fuel' conference and speak on behalf of your company to elaborate on your company's vision and achievements with respect to this agenda. The most important thing about this type of public speaking is that you need to have a lot of company knowledge and understanding. You can prepare a brilliant speech on the topic being discussed, only to be tripped up by questions at the end of your session which focus on your company and its mission, vision or history. Make sure that before your undertake this type of speaking that you speak to someone in your PR or media office, if you have one, since they will be able to ensure you have all the background information you need. They will also flag to you any areas that should not be discussed in a public setting – especially with journalists.

The final type of public speaking is that of *hosting an event*. This is where you are the person who opens the event, introduces speakers and closes the event. You are the person who controls the entrance and exit of key speakers within their alloted times, and you also have the overall responsibility of ensuring that everyone continues to be engaged throughout the event. Hosting an event is a bit more challenging than purely speaking on behalf of your company, or speaking on behalf of yourself, because it introduces elements of event management and speaker engagement. After all, if a speaker is running over his or her allotted time, you cannot just interrupt them with the exclamation that their time is up and they need to stop now. You will need to be sensitive to the audience and the speaker – sometimes you can observe that it would be beneficial to let this speaker continue for another five minutes and shorten the lunch by five minutes, or you may pick up that the audience is getting restless and you need to intervene.

Other differences between types of public speaking

Another point to consider for a speaker is the motivation of the audience in being there, since this can make a big difference to how successful your speech may or may not be. Many people attend a public speaking event out of personal or business interest, and are eager (to varying extents!) to hear the information being shared. However, sometimes people attend events because they are required to do so rather than because they want to. For example, an employee may be required to attend a conference on behalf of his company, or a student may be required to attend as a credit requirement for a course of study. In these situations, these members of your audience are less likely to be enthusiastic about the speech you are going to give. If you are not cognisant of these people, your confidence may be severely compromised when you find that they are not responding to what you feel is a good and valuable discussion. I will discuss this in more detail in the chapter covering researching your audience.

How do people on the spectrum generally handle the various types of public speaking?

Let us now consider how we – as individuals on the autistic spectrum – may react to each of the types of public speaking.

Speaking on behalf of yourself as a specialist or professional

I have spoken about this in Chapter 2 and so I will not go into too much detail here. Suffice to say that this is the type of public speaking where people on the autistic spectrum do tend to excel, since our levels of knowledge and passion can be extremely high when speaking on a topic of particular interest to us. Here we can very much focus on what we know best, and are generally able to pull together our presentations in a way that suits us. Unlike generic business speaking events, those events focusing around particular interests tend to have audiences who are almost as passionate (and sometimes even as passionate!) about the topic as we are. This makes having empathy with the audience far easier. In addition, it is also far easier to become so engrossed in our topic of interest and sharing what we know, that we completely overcome any fears and pre-speech nerves. As a result we frequently come across as confident and knowledgable experts, whereas most neurotypicals would not be able to distance themselves so easily from their public speaking fears and nerves if they suffer from them, no matter how interested they are in the topic. However, the only area where we do not have a natural advantage is in respect of being a charismatic speaker. While this may come naturally to some people, it is not a generic strength of those on the spectrum.

As a result, this type of public speaking suits most of us extremely well. If you are thinking about starting to speak publicly in this area, I hope that this book will ensure that you not only come across as confident and knowledgable, but also leave a lasting impression on your listeners by being a charismatic speaker.

Academic speaking

In academic speaking, the largest area of importance for the audience is that of knowledge and, as already mentioned, this can be a particular strength for those of us on the spectrum. Of course, being able to present in a manner that is engaging and captivating will make the event more memorable for the academics taking part, but their main focus will be the information you would be sharing. For many of us on the spectrum, academic speaking is actually equivalent to speaking on your specialist topic. The only time that this may differ slightly is where you are possibly employed by or lecturing with a university, for example, where this type of public speaking may overlap into the area of speaking on behalf of your organisation.

Internal presentations to your team

Although many neurotypicals consider presenting to their internal teams as pretty straight-forward, for some people on the spectrum this can be seen as even more of a challenge than doing an external presentation, because in this scenario you are presenting to people you know and work with. When you present to your internal team, it is important that you do this formally rather than the way you would ordinarily communicate with them. It can feel challenging or artificial to suddenly stand up and present to them with a 'different hat' if you have not prepared adequately for this.

Internal presentations to your company

As with internal presentations to your team, some may consider this not as intense an undertaking as speaking to a broader audience, albeit that it may be more challenging than just speaking to your own team. In general, this tends to be true for people on the spectrum as well. If you hold a senior position in the business, it is likely that most people in the organisation will know who you are. It is therefore easier to present more 'naturally' to this audience than you would to a group of strangers. Nevertheless, if you are not familiar with how to do formal business presentations, you may find that some preparation beforehand could stand you in good stead. For example, I know a number of people (both neurotypical and spectrumites) who are really surprised to discover that their presentations do not go down well because of factors such as speaking too softly, not making eye contact, making too many gestures or hand movements, or being too direct. These are the kinds of topics that will be covered in the chapters of preparing yourself for public speaking.

Speaking on behalf of your company at a public event

When you undertake a speaking engagement to the general public rather than people or organisations you know or are relatively familiar with, you may well struggle with issues relating to sensory overload (which can be significantly amplified by the environment you are undertaking the speaking event in) as well as feeling daunted by how you are supposed to present yourself and also network with people afterwards. Many of the chapters in this book deal with some of the very specific situations you may encounter as a business leader speaking on behalf of your company, so this should help you to overcome any challenges you may experience.

Hosting an event

Hosting an event is very much about introducing speakers and topics, but it is also about time management and control. This part of hosting can be challenging for those of us on the spectrum, because it is very much about observing reactions and acting appropriately. Throughout the book I emphasise the importance of working with and trying to empathise with the audience and include tools to help you achieve this.

As the breakdown reflects, while the phrase 'public speaking' tends to come with a single mental image for most people, there are several very different types of public speaking, some of which you may be better at than others. To ensure that you can be the best speaker you can, it is important that you are not only aware of the different types of speaking, but that you have strategies to cope with the varying requirements to undertake each one. As you progress through this book, we will be talking about the various types of speaking and some of the challenges you may face as you undertake them. I use the word 'challenge' here as opposed to difficulties or issues, since these challenges can be successfully overcome in order for you to undertake the type of public speaking that will make a positive impact and leave a lasting impression. As you work through the book, do try to complete as many of the toolkits as you can, even if you feel that they may not be appropriate for you at that particular time. As I said in the previous chapter, you never know when you are going to be required to speak publicly, and therefore preparation is never a waste of time.

Chapter 4

Early Coping Strategies

If you have never spoken publicly before, you may be experiencing mixed feelings at the prospect of doing so for the first time. Some people can be really excited by the thought, others may be horrified. Some sit in between the two extremes. Whatever your personal experience at the thought of undertaking your public speaking debut, there are a number of things you can do in preparation for this that will help you have a positive and encouraging experience.

The first thing to discuss in more detail is the way people do experience their event on actually reaching it. You will be surprised at the number of people who eagerly and confidently await the arrival of their public speaking event, only to be so overcome by nerves or downright fear that they are unable to get up on the stage, or if they do, they struggle to complete their speech in any intelligent manner due to the adrenaline pumping through their veins causing trembling legs, dry mouths and shaking voices.

At the other extreme, there are people who worry endlessly about the upcoming event, only to fly through their actual speech effortlessly and with great enjoyment – much to their surprise and delight.

My aim in this chapter is to help you to be a position to encompass the best of both of the two scenarios above. I want you to be confident and eager for your engagement, and also undertake it successfully and with great enjoyment. Public speaking should be something that you really enjoy, not a task as such. In order for it to be that, however, there needs to be some preparation for those of us on the spectrum, perhaps a bit more so than for neurotypicals.

How will I react?

Part of understanding how you need to prepare yourself for public speaking is to understand what types of reactions you experience when you are ready to step up on the podium and why you are experiencing them. There are a number of different responses your body may present you with at this time, including:

- sweating

- shaking and trembling

- nausea

- feeling you need to go to the bathroom (when you don't!)

- shaking voice

- loss of voice

- 'brain-dead' syndrome – where we go completely blank, cannot remember a single thing you were going to speak about

- general panic attack, where we start breathing too fast, flood our bodies with oxygen and as a consequence feel we cannot breathe.

All of the above physical reactions can be recognised as the general responses of the body to fear. Yes, the thought of speaking publicly actually frighten us. After all, worry can be considered a derivative of fear!

For people on the spectrum there are some additional responses we could experience which are unique to our being on the spectrum, and it is important that we consider these as well. First let me speak about how we, as people on the autistic spectrum, actually handle stress.

How do people on the autistic spectrum generally react to stress?

This is a highly personal and individually variable topic. The way stress affects one person on the spectrum could differ considerably from the way it affects another. I am looking at some of the generic causes for any challenges we may experience. Remember that the degree to which these apply to you depends on how well you currently cope with stress, how much exposure you have had to it in the past, and some of your individual sensory and cognitive challenges and strengths.

In order to give some thought to how you react to stressors, complete the first part of Toolkit Exercise 3: Early Coping Strategies (p.155) in Part 5 of the book.

Sensory overload

Most of us on the autistic spectrum have one or more hypersensitivities. For anyone who is not aware of what this is, it means that we have one or more overly sensitive perceptive senses, be it hearing, eyesight, smell, touch or taste, which are subject to overload due to too much input (Attwood 2007). Unlike neurotypicals, when we start to receive too much input to one of our hypersensitive senses, this creates the build-up of tension ultimately ending in an overload experience. When I first tried to understand how this differed from neurotypicals, the one thing that I realised after speaking to people was that for a neurotypical, removing oneself from an environment that was uncomfortable resulted in the discomfort immediately ceasing. For example, if someone turned on the radio and it was playing painfully loud, all they needed to do was turn the volume down and then things would be back to normal. We are generally not so fortunate. Let's take the same example. We turn on a radio and the volume is painfully loud. We immediately turn off the radio, but the pain and sensation of those voluminous sound-waves continue to resound through us for an hour before they finally dissipate.

I like to visualise this as what I call the funnel effect. Neurotypicals have an open channel through which they can receive sensory information (see Figure 4.1).

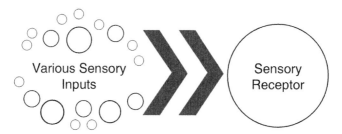

Figure 4.1 Neurotypical sensory perception

Once they reach the point where the sensory information is too much, they can close the channel and any residual sensory data will dissipate into the surrounding area. For those of us with an autistic spectrum disorder, however, sensory information reaches us through what I see as a funnel that focuses and intensifies that information before it enters the sensory system (see Figure 4.2). Because our sensory system is hypersensitive, it means that the brain is making information 'manageable' by effectively slowing it down. In the situation where there is too much sensory data coming in, the funnel becomes blocked. If the sensory input is terminated, rather than any residual data dissipating into the surrounding area, this is held in place by the walls of the funnel and hence continues to enter. The excess data will therefore only really stop affecting us after it has had the chance to be compressed into the funnel and finally into our sensory system.

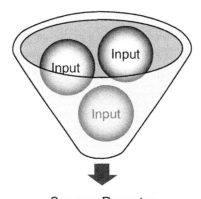

Sensory Receptor

Figure 4.2 Asperger sensory perception

It is during this period of time when we cannot escape from the effects of the excessive input that we tend to experience sensory overload. Effects of this differ per individual, but can include things such as headaches, panic attacks, inability to speak, inability to communicate, emotional outbursts and even the activation of co-morbid (or co-existing) conditions, such as epilepsy or asthma.

Need for time alone

Frequently as a result of sensory overload issues, we need periods of time alone to recuperate. Coping with overloads or even just the 'business as usual' coping strategies takes a lot of effort, and we require time apart from others to recover our energies. In a period of stress, this need for personal time increases as it takes longer for us to recover.

Hypervigilance

It is not surprising that people who have hypersensitivities tend to experience hypervigilance. This is when we are acutely aware of our surroundings and constantly on a look-out for things that can be perceived as threats, especially when we have recently had an overload experience. For example, someone with visual hypersensitivity could have experienced a recent overload due to trying to give a presentation in a venue with a faulty spotlight that kept flashing in her eyes. The next time she goes to undertake a speaking engagement, that same individual is likely to be overly tense and observant regarding anything to do with the lights or visual stimuli.

Loss of focus

It is interesting to read about the concept of what is termed monotropism (Murray, Lester and Lawson 2005). Monotropism is where we pay attention to or perceive detail, but struggle with seeing the big picture or whole. Attwood (2007) refers to this as weak central cohesion. My belief about successful people with Asperger syndrome and careers is that we have been able to develop strategies to redress this shortfall quite early in our school life, and that we have quite adept central coherence by the time we start our careers. I would be the last to say that we do not still have the propensity to get stuck in the detail, as you would have seen from what I have been discussing in the book so far. However, I believe it to be an area we have of necessity worked hard to compensate for.

There is one example provided by Tony Attwood (2007), however, that I personally do not agree with. In discussing the subject of weak central cohesion, Attwood describes our attention to details as being similar to a person looking at the world through a rolled up piece of paper, hence not seeing a lot of information. I dare to counter that example. I believe that actually we tend to see a lot more detail than most people. Far from seeing only a restricted view through the rolled up paper, we see everything. Let me give you my own example for this. Imagine a situation where a family is sitting in their lounge. Suddenly they hear an unusual noise outside. In the one scenario, the father asks his neurotypical son to have a look outside and tell them what he sees. The son goes to the window and feeds back that he sees nothing – he has perceived that everything looks normal. In the second scenario, the father asks his Asperger son to look outside and tell them what he sees. The son goes to the window and feeds back that he sees the following: it is sunny, there is a light breeze that is moving the leaves on the trees nearby, there is a squirrel on the pathway, there are a number of cumulus clouds developing, there is a small fly caught in a spider's web on the outside of the window, there is a pair of turtle doves on the bush nearby… We do not see part of the picture outside the window, we see everything. Where we have a challenge is actually determining from that information what is relevant and what isn't. In the above example, the neurotypical son had attuned to look for something out of the ordinary, and therefore filtered out anything irrelevant. The son with Asperger's was not able to do this effectively.

As we have grown, we have developed techniques to recognise what we need to focus on and what we need to ignore or put aside to process later. Unlike neurotypicals, we do not automatically filter information. It is something we need to learn to do. By the time we have reached high school, this is generally something we can do quite effectively in normal circumstances.

However, in situations of stress, we may find that we become more distracted by irrelevant information. In a way, we regress to a situation where we could be having a conversation with someone about a very important topic only to interrupt ourselves midsentence to comment on the colour of butterfly that just flew past, or be totally distracted from a speech we are giving by an unusual hairstyle of someone in the audience.

Shutdowns

Shutdowns can often occur as a result of sensory overload. As a means to cut out this overwhelming bombardment of information and sensory data, we teach ourselves to block out the world. We switch off or shutdown. Sometimes we do this by totally ceasing to function, by going into our room and staring into space. However, for most of us, one of the ways we do this is to become totally engrossed in something. At work, this could mean that we sit down in front of our computer and effectively shut out the rest of the office. We don't hear, see or feel anything other than the computer. We are in a bubble.

In times of stress, we may find that we are starting to do this more frequently. We end up distancing ourselves from others unintentionally, and can be seen as ignoring the people around us.

Perfectionism

Many of us experience a level of personal perfectionism in areas where we believe we can do well. Our thinking tends to be black or white, and therefore we tend to see our own performance as either good or bad. As people on the autistic spectrum, we tend to put a high value on the concept of intelligence (I discuss this more fully in one of my other books, *An Asperger Leader's Guide to Living and Leading Change*, 2013). Generally, this is because we see it as an area in which we are not hindered by any developmental disorders, and have not had to struggle with as much as other areas, such as social and communication skills. We obtain a lot of our sense of worth from our ability to perform well. Any perception on our part that we are underperforming can cause great frustration and stress for us.

During times of stress we can end up becoming overly perfectionistic about whatever it is we are doing. If we are preparing a speech, this means that we may end up being so particular about exactly what we are saying, the order it is said, the materials we use, the visuals we may have to develop, the way we should present it and so forth, that we never actually finish preparing the speech by the time the day of your speech arrives.

Order and routine

Almost everyone with an autistic spectrum disorder craves order and routine. Most of us, however, have learnt to find ways to ensure that this predisposition does not become an undue focus for us. But when a situation becomes stressful, we can revert to needing order and routine around us. We can end up spending significant amounts of time ordering our desks, or categorising projects, or developing a new labelling technique for our calendars, rather than getting on with what we are supposed to be doing. Similarly, we may develop an increased tendency to rigidly adhere to the rules and established procedures during times of stress, far more than we ordinarily would.

Stimming

Stimming (abbreviated from the word stimulating) is where we undertake some kind of repetitive physical activity aimed at focusing our attention away from a stressor and therefore bringing that stress under control. Examples of stimming would include rapid finger tapping, rapid toe or foot tapping, rocking, humming, finger or hand flapping or bouncing in one's seat. As with most things, stimming is highly individual. For those of us who have been in business for a long time, we have either learnt to suppress any stimming, or to convert to a type of stimming which is more socially acceptable. However, when a situation becomes stressful, it is highly likely that stimming may increase, or you may inadvertently revert to what you may consider your less favourable stimming methods.

Triggers of co-morbid conditions such as asthma or epilepsy

Many of us have medical conditions that exist together with our autism, conditions which are called co-morbid medical conditions. Some of the most common are asthma and epilepsy. When we get particularly stressed, there is a risk of these conditions playing up, and as a result we may have to take more medication or be more careful.

But I have developed coping strategies already – can't I make use of them?

Most of us on the autistic spectrum have spent a large part of our lives internalising coping strategies as we have grown up and progressed to various stages in our lives and careers. For many of us, these coping strategies are what have helped us to be successful in our education, jobs and personal lives. Without any doubt, you are likely to make use of some of your coping strategies when you start to speak publicly, but some of those strategies may not be optimal for a public speaking environment.

Here is an example to explain what I mean by this. In my own life, one of my coping strategies when I reach a point of overload is to distance myself from the situation. So, if I find that I am being overwhelmed by too many personal interactions in the workplace, I go for fifteen minutes to my quiet place where there are no other people around, and where – if the overload is particularly bad – I can switch off the lights and sit in the dark. In most situations this coping strategy can be adapted to work to varying degrees. So if, for example, I am at a client's office where I do not have my own quiet space, I will excuse myself to go to the bathroom and sit in a cubicle for a few minutes. I am sure most of you can think of similar ways in which you have adapted your coping strategy for the situation you find yourself in.

However, it is actually extremely difficult to adapt that particular coping strategy to a public speaking environment. After all, you are standing in front of an audience, and you cannot just excuse yourself to go and get some quiet time. In this case the coping strategy does not work. There are a number of potential coping strategies that do not – practically – work in a public speaking environment. Others may seem to still be applicable, but when you think about it, they can have unexpected side-effects. Think about another coping strategy used by a number of people – some form of tapping. Sometimes people are able to control stress levels by doing something like tapping a surface with their fingers, or tapping their leg or even tapping their temple or forehead. Now, while it may appear that this is something you could still do in a public speaking environment, this can have the unwanted side-effect of distracting your audience, to the extent that they end up not recalling the details of your speech, but rather your mannerisms during the speech. There is nothing I hate to hear more than when I ask someone what they thought of speech, than responses to the effect of: 'Yeah, that speaker was really weird! He kept tapping his leg with his right hand…' If you ask again about the speech and what it was about and/or like, quite frequently they will give you quite a broad answer, showing that they really did not internalise what the speaker had been trying to share.

Now is a good time to complete the second part of Toolkit Exercise 3: Early Coping Strategies in Part 5 of the book (Your current coping strategies p.157). This will help you consider whether your current coping strategies are still relevant.

You may feel a little alarmed. After all, if you cannot effectively use your coping strategies, just what should you be doing?

Developing or adapting your coping strategies for public speaking

As mentioned earlier, developing coping strategies for anything involves two steps:

1. Understanding the reason we need a coping strategy for a certain event. If we are going to develop a coping strategy for something that causes us to have a negative reaction, we need first of all to understand what it is about that event or phenomenon that actually causes us to have that negative reaction.

2. Developing a coping strategy that will effectively address what we have identified as the reason for needing the coping strategy in step 1.

Here is an example:

Case Study: Muhammad's fear of the City

Muhammad Arid was a finance clerk working at a large financial institute in Peterborough, England. Muhammad loved his job and felt that it was a field he was very effective in. One day, he was offered a promotion within his company that required him to relocate to London. Muhammad thought about the opportunity and spent some time coming to terms with the fact that this would mean he would have to move to a new flat and get to know a new environment. This was the only thing that made him hesitate in accepting the offer. However, his eagerness to grow in his career eventually helped him overcome his fear of change, and he accepted the promotion and made arrangements to move to London within the next two months.

His company had a very supportive programme for people being promoted to head office roles from the regions, and therefore he was able to get a suitable flat for himself in Wimbledon, just outside London, through their relocation service provider.

On arriving at his new apartment, having taken two weeks relocation leave to orientate himself to the area, Muhammad spent time getting to know his new environment in Wimbledon itself. He was pleased with the facilities in his apartment building and how comfortable he felt in the Wimbledon area itself. By the time he was due to start working at the London head office, he felt almost completely settled.

On his first working day, Muhammad took the underground train into London for the first time. By the time he reached his office in Canary Wharf in London's financial mile, he was stressed and beginning to experience an overload. He hurried to the high-rise building housing his employer and made his way to human resources as he had been asked to do. Eventually he had completed the condensed induction and was shown to his department.

Muhammad was rather taken aback by the size of the bank itself and the number of people in each department. In Peterborough, the bank was situated in an old historic building, consisting of a network of offices over only three floors. The finance department was split into a number of offices, and his team had been in a large office containing eight desks, each separated by dividers, making each desk area into a cubicle.

In the London office, however, the entire floor space on each floor was open plan. There were easily one hundred people in Muhammad's area alone, all working at long, open plan desks with no dividers between them. For Muhammad, this came as an incredible shock. However, his manager and the people he was working with all seemed to be very nice and supportive individuals, and he felt he could work well with them.

By early afternoon, Muhammad felt himself starting to have an asthma attack. He was really surprised, since he had not had an attack in over five years. Fortunately, he did still carry his asthma pump, and he was able to make use of it, but for the remainder of the day he felt light-headed and dizzy.

On his second day at the office, he reached the office already feeling his chest tightening up and his head reeling. Much as he tried to ignore what he was experiencing, every day that he was at work the symptoms seemed to get worse and worse, to the point that Muhammad actually wondered whether he would be able to continue to work there.

On the Friday, he made contact with a friend he had in Peterborough, Emma, who happened to be a psychologist, and arranged to meet with her the following day. Sitting together, Muhammad shared what had been happening with her. He shared how difficult it was for him to go to work every day, and how he struggled to use some of the coping strategies that he had previously developed, because they no longer seemed to be working.

'Tell me, Muhammad,' Emma said, 'What do you think it is that is causing the problem?'

Muhammad shook his head despondently as he took a sip of his coffee.

'I believe I just have a phobia of the City, that's all. I just can't work there. It is too big.'

Emma nodded.

'So when did you say you arrived there?'

'Just over three weeks ago now.'

'And what do you think of your new home?'

'It's really nice. I feel like I fit in there really well.'

Emma smiled.

'Well, that's good news. Did you spend some time out and about getting to know the area?'

'Oh yes, it was great.'

'And did you go into London?'

'Yes, I took the bus in because I hadn't bought an Oyster card for the underground yet. There are some lovely restaurants there.'

'Yes there are, and some fascinating historical buildings.'

'Oh yes, I absolutely loved Trafalgar Square…'

Emma and Muhammad sat quietly for a few moments before Emma asked Muhammad a question he was not expecting.

'So, Muhammad, if you think that the reason you have been having an overload is because London is just too big, why do you think you didn't have one when you went to visit it before starting work?'

Muhammad stared at Emma for a few minutes, confused.

'I don't know,' he muttered eventually, 'I hadn't thought about that.'

'Okay,' Emma prompted. 'So what was different about your visits to London before you started working to those since you have been working?'

Muhammad frowned.

'Well, I didn't have to go to work, first of all. I wasn't wearing my work clothes. I didn't have any time pressures. I wasn't thinking about work issues…'

'Can I suggest something else?' Emma interjected. 'How did you get to London?'

'Well, as I said, I took the bus.'

'And how have you been travelling to work since you started work?'

'I have been taking the tube of course – it is much quicker in the morning.'

'Mmmmm.'

Muhammad looked at Emma, picking up on her pause. He thought about what she had just asked him. He had taken the underground. But when he had gone into London and had no problems, he had taken the bus… Muhammad looked up at Emma in surprise.

'Are you saying it's because I took the tube? Could it be that I have a problem with the tube, not with the City itself?'

Emma smiled.

'Well, you know that if you have an overload issue first thing in the morning it can last all day, especially if you have no strategies to get it under control. Does your overload dissipate once you get home?'

'No!' Muhammad said, as if realising something for the first time. 'No. It gets worse. That was what I couldn't understand!'

'Well, if you have just had another tube ride to get home, that's hardly surprising, is it? Can I suggest that for the next couple of weeks you take the bus into work and back, and see what difference that makes to your overloads? If it does seem to improve things, we will know what your actual trigger is and can talk about some coping strategies for if you need to use the underground any time in the future.' Muhammad felt a ray of hope rising in his chest. Perhaps he wasn't having a reaction to the City as such, but just to a particular mode of transport. Perhaps he could continue to work in London after all.

As you can see from the above example, Muhammad was unable to address the problems he was experiencing in London until he was able to find out the actual reason for having an adverse reaction. This is equally valid for any of us, in any situation. If you find that you are having some sort of reaction – be it a panic attack or some sort of sensory overload – it is essential you determine exactly what is causing it before trying to determine a coping strategy. You could be trying to use a strategy aimed at calming your reaction to something completely different (such as a reaction to a large city versus a reaction to the confined space of the underground); therefore the strategy could be completely the opposite of what you need.

Looking at our public speaking scenario, in order to determine the root cause of any negative reactions we may be having, the first question you need to ask yourself is 'How do I react when I speak publicly?' If you have already undertaken some speaking, you will know the answer to that. However, even if you are certain that you do know, it is always worthwhile getting an outside opinion! Frequently, there are things that happen to us if we are nervous about speaking that we are not even aware of. Therefore, it is worthwhile asking someone to observe you making some form of presentation so that they can feed back to you your presentation or speaking style and mannerisms.

If you can, take the opportunity to speak at some different venues and see if you experience anything that you want to address going forward. If you do, consider what may have caused the problem. Was it related to the environment? The stage? The lighting? Or was it something like starting at the front with all eyes trained on you?

I hope that the Toolkit Exercises you have completed so far will have given you insight into some of the areas you as an individual may experience as challenges when it comes to public speaking, and any coping strategies you may need to review. No problem is insurmountable. Many people who were initially some of the most nervous and inhibited speakers have moved on to become successful presenters following some development. I am confident that the targeted development tools presented here will make a difference.

Let's go back now to what I was discussing at the beginning of the chapter, namely that many physical reactions we experience when speaking publicly are just our reactions to the emotion of fear. What we are experiencing, whether we recognise it or not, is a fear of public speaking. In order to develop some coping strategies for our specific overload issues, we first of all need to understand the causes of the general fears and make sure that these do not end up stimulating our unique overload areas.

Understanding the fear of public speaking

Psychologists refer to this fear as communication anxiety, and it is by no means unusual. In fact, most speakers experience this to varying degrees. So what is it about public speaking that raises the emotion of fear within us? In general, there are five areas that people tend to be concerned about before they speak:

- that they will embarrass themselves

- that they will not live up to their own standards

- that they will lose the respect of important people in their lives

- that they will lose the respect of the public in general

- that they will jeopardise their career going forward.

Fear of embarrassing yourself

This is understandably the most common fear that people have ahead of speaking. Their fear that they are going to embarrass themselves can cause people to imagine all sorts of things, from messing up on the words to tripping and falling on the stage. Your mind is a very powerful instrument. If we allow it to have free rein on our thoughts relating to how we could embarrass ourselves, it is amazing how many possible scenarios it can come up with!

Fear of embarrassing yourself is very closely tied to a focus on yourself rather than your audience or the purpose of your engagement. A key part of addressing this fear is to turn your focus outwards towards your audience. Your key SPEAK skill here is *empathy* – focus on them and not on you.

Not living up to your own standards

I would say that this is by far the most prevalent concern among people on the autistic spectrum when it comes to speaking publicly. We tend to set very high standards for ourselves and take it very personally if we fail to live up to our expectations. This is linked to our tendency towards perfectionism, especially when we become stressed. The risk of setting our standards too high due to underlying perfectionism is that we will end up making the feedback from the audience far more important than it should be. What I mean by this is that while we should value feedback from the audience and seek to use it to improve our future presentations if necessary, what we should not be doing is making that one set of feedback end up determining our speaking career. If you receive some feedback that the event was not quite what they expected, for example, if you are perfectionist this can totally overtake any other positive feedback and make you think you are a failure.

Let me give you a personal example from a number of years back. I was invited to speak at an international event on a specialist topic. Given that it was international, this was done as a web-conference so that people could watch and interact over the internet. At the end of the conference the participants were asked for their feedback on my speech. While the majority of the feedback was very positive, giving me a very high score and making additional comments about how good the information was, one participant came back with a low score saying that although the information was useful, he didn't think I was that engaging. To say that I was devastated is an understatement. I totally took that comment to heart, completely overlooking the positive (and extremely complementary) ones. I felt that this was a true reflection of me as a speaker – that I was a poor speaker because I did not engage appropriately. It was only when I was speaking to an associate later that he chastised me for my negative thinking. 'Haven't you even read the other comments?' he asked. At this point I stopped and went back to the feedback page and started to re-read the other feedback. The overall impression from the audience was actually that I had done an excellent presentation and that they would be interested in future engagements I was speaking at. But I was so overwhelmed by the negative message from one person who challenged my extremely high standards, that I totally blanked this out.

Fear of losing the respect of important others in your life

This is such a sad fear if you think about it. Do we really think that people who care about us would lose respect for us if we do not deliver the perfect speech? This ties in to our self-image in some ways, since if we were more confident in how other people perceived us and accepted us for who we are, then we would be less concerned that one unsuccessful speaking event (should the event even be unsuccessful) would result in the loss of their respect.

Fear of losing the respect of the public in general

People will always fear that if they make a speech that is not perfect, people who came to watch them will be disappointed and ultimately lose any respect they had for them as a speaker. The reality is that most people coming to watch you speak are expecting you to succeed. Unless you drop your notes and run out of the conference hall crying, it is highly unlikely they would notice if your speech does not quite reach the standards you had set yourself. It will, in all likelihood, meet their expectations, and that is what matters. Even if the speech was not 100 per cent what they had expected, most people are well aware that there are good days and there are bad days, and that just because the speech had a flaw or two does not mean that the person is flawed themselves!

Fear of jeopardising your future career

If you are speaking on behalf of your company at an event, there is often the fear that if you do anything less than a perfect speech you will be putting your career at the company at risk. Fortunately, this is a very unlikely scenario. Unless you make a massive error that totally undermines or threatens the company in some way, it is very unlikely that your speech would have such a drastic effect. On the other hand, if you know you are going to be asked to speak regularly on behalf of your company and this is something you struggle with, then it is worthwhile getting some individual coaching in advance so that you can feel more confident in your abilities – more for your peace of mind than anyone else's.

Some additional coping strategies based on social communication anxiety

Coping strategies are highly unique to the people who use them, since they need to be developed to address that individual's specific area of challenge. However, there are some generic coping strategies that I can share with you as another individual on the spectrum who makes use of them when needed. These relate to the effects of social communication anxiety (or fear of public speaking) rather than any particular sensory overload issues.

- *Changing your perceptions* – The most important coping strategy for overcoming social communication anxiety is to change the way you perceive public speaking. For those people who experience stress reactions to public speaking, you will often hear them make the statement that 'the mere thought of it' makes them stressed. This is totally understandable, since our thoughts are some of the most powerful assets (or weaknesses!) we can have when it comes to handling stress.

  However, many of the reactions that we have to public speaking are physiological reactions to a perceived stressor or threat, such as sweating, shaking, palpitations and so forth. Part of overcoming your physical reactions is to change your perception of the actual speaking event. Complete Toolkit Exercise 4: Changing Perceptions of Public Speaking (p.164) in Part 5.

- *Changing your self-talk* – Again, this is very closely linked to how strongly our internal perceptions can influence our thinking. 'Self-talk' refers to those ongoing thoughts we tend to have in our heads, and whether or not they are positive or negative.

Let's look at some of the most common negative self-talk that potential public speakers could have rolling around in their heads. They could be thinking things such as:

- 'I really know nothing about public speaking – I'm an amateur.'
- 'I don't really have anything special to offer.'
- 'I'm bound to mess up – I always do.'

The mind is a very powerful tool, and when we hear these sentiments over and over again, they will eventually become an integral part of our internal belief system. However, instead of these negative thoughts, what we should be replacing them with are the positive ones that can encourage and reinforce our positive self-image. Examples are:

- 'I am a specialist in my field and people want to hear from me.'
- 'The chances of me messing up are minimal – I am well prepared.'
- 'I have something really unique to offer.'

Keeping this sort of narrative in your mind will help you to internalise your value to your potential audience, and enable you to step forward confidently when the time comes.

- *Breathing and stretching exercises* – Breathing and stretching exercises are very practical tools that can be used at the time of your event as well as before and after it. The breathing exercises are based on slowing down your breathing. Take a deep breath and hold it for ten seconds. Then slowly release your breath, blowing it out of your mouth through pinched lips (almost as if you were going to whistle). Repeat this exercise a couple of times. You should find that your heart rate slows down and you begin to feel more relaxed.

  If you are able to do them, stretching exercises are also very useful to release tension in your muscles. The most helpful stretches are for your arms and neck. Some stretches for your arms are:

  - Reach up over your head with your right arm while keeping your left by your side. Hold it there for a few seconds. Then repeat the exercise for your left arm. This has the effect of loosening the muscles in your back as well as releasing tension in your upper arms.

  - Lift your right arm so that it is at a 45 degree angle to the ground and pointed straight ahead of you. With your left arm, take hold of your right elbow and gently pull your arm towards the left side of your body. Hold it there for a couple of seconds. Gently release your arm and move it back to its natural position. Repeat the exercise for your left arm. This has the effect of loosening the muscles around your shoulders and neck as well as working on your back.

Other stretches that are useful are head rolls and jaw stretches.

- *Tapping* – Tapping is a technique that I have found particularly useful, and I think many people on the spectrum may well have the same experience. I am certainly not an expert on the topic, and therefore will not be going into a lot of detail here, but I certainly do recommend you read about this. I have included some details of additional reading on this in Further Reading.

  In summary, however, tapping is a proven technique where certain pressure points in the body are stimulated (or destimulated) by tapping different areas of the body with your fingertips. Tapping is actually a nickname for the actual technique called EFT (Emotional Freedom Technique) and it works by allowing you to reconnect your mind with your body's messages and vice versa. In a way, I would see this as a variation on acupuncture, but with one main difference. It is something completely in your control and a technique you can use by yourself in isolation – and with no needles in sight!

  My interest was aroused when I first read about tapping techniques because of an experience I had had many years ago. My parents had previously tried acupuncture as a way to get me under control when I was a teenager (their not knowing – or knowing and not accepting – at that time that I was autistic). I found that pressure applied to certain areas had exactly the opposite effect on me that it was supposed to. For example, I was being given a session whereby the acupuncturist applied the equipment and then left the room. As I waited for him to return I started to get more and more tense. By the time he returned a few minutes later I was ready to scream, all my muscles being tense and my body shaking. The man was really surprised, saying that he had expected me to be asleep, since the areas he had activated were meant to relax people. Well, obviously not for me!

  When I read about tapping, I was understandably suspicious, given the above experience. However, I realised that I have always used my own form of tapping to control my tension when I get tense. When I get stressed, I tap the left side of my forehead with my finger and eventually this will resolve the tension. What peaked my interest was that the book I was reading said that one of the techniques was to tap the right side of your forehead to relieve tension – the exact opposite of what I found useful personally.

The nice thing about tapping is that this is something that you can experiment with yourself. It is something you do and therefore you can take the time to find out what works for you. You may find that it doesn't help at all, but if you do find that it helps, it can be a very handy tool.

What I have found particularly useful is that you can also teach yourself to apply the principles of tapping through the equivalent of visualisation as described in Part 5 Toolkit Exercise 4 Part 1: Understanding your current reactions using visualisation (p.164). By doing this you potentially have a coping strategy that you can apply whether you are in the public sight or not, whereas other strategies are more difficult to do in front of other people.

If you think this is something that could be beneficial to you, I would strongly recommend that you read the book *Step-by-Step Tapping* by Sue Beer and Emma Roberts (2013).

These coping strategies are some that you can practise putting into place well ahead of your speaking engagement, so that they come naturally to you by the time you need to speak.

PART 2

Key Elements for Successful Public Speaking

Chapter 5

Developing Your Public Speaking Persona

What do I mean by a public speaking persona?

Public speaking involves more than just standing up and talking about something. In order for public speaking to be effective, it is essential that you not only use your voice effectively, but your body, personality and mannerisms as well. When you are speaking publicly, you may end up emphasising, or using certain elements of how you speak more and other elements less. This 'character' you let people see is your public speaking persona.

Let's clarify the above with a thought experiment. Have you ever been to an event where there have been a number of speakers, some of whom you found appealing and some of whom you really did not enjoy listening to? Take a few moments now to think back on some of those speakers and consider just what it was that made them either appealing or the opposite. For many people on the spectrum, we will probably say that what made a speaker appealing was the relevance of what he or she had to say. This isn't unusual for us. We tend to deal in the 'fact and figures' of public speaking – if someone is speaking about something that is of particular interest to us, we aren't that fussed about the manner in which they present it – unless, of course, they speak in such a way that is illogical or causes a sensory overload!

For most neurotypicals, however, how appealing a presentation comes across is intricately linked to how engaging the speaker is: does the speaker make eye contact? Does he or she make appropriate jokes and get the audience relaxed? Does he or she vary their voice at appropriate times to make speech less mundane? Is he or she animated? Does he or she use their body and face in such a way that it draws the listener in?

Now, I recognise that many of these questions are ones that we just would not think to consider. Why would we be interested in jokes, for example? Surely that is an irritating diversion? Well, for us maybe. For neurotypicals –

absolutely not! The reality is that when we are speaking publicly – especially if we are speaking on behalf of our companies – it is highly likely that the majority (if not all) of our audience will be neurotypical. The importance of this for you is that you will need to ensure that any speaking you do reflects a public speaking persona that people can identify with and feel comfortable with.

At this point some people become quite confused about the underlying purpose of developing a speaking persona.

'Surely that's the same as pretending to be someone I am not?' you may ask.

Not really. This is the development of your public face – the key parts of you that you want to emphasise and optimise. Certainly, for those of us with ASD, this may include learning some skills that are not intrinsic, but I would remind you that this skill is something that you would have had to do as part of your learning to fit in at school and at work as well. For most of us it is not a foreign concept. However, I strongly recommend that your speaking persona truly reflects who you are as a person on the autistic spectrum, complemented by the presentation skills you will learn in this book – as opposed to someone who presents an artificial face to cover your true nature. I consider that being autistic is an asset rather than a weakness, and yet I do also make sure that I develop my skills in areas where I know that I am perhaps not as strong or conversant as neurotypical people.

As I mentioned in Chapter 2, people make an impact in their speaking through the elements of SPEAK, namely:

- *Self-knowledge* – Having an understanding of your own personal speaking style, areas that make you unique, and a full understanding of and mechanism to apply any necessary coping or adjustment techniques that are all your own.

- *Passion and charisma* – Feeling impassioned about what you are speaking about and being able to captivate your audience and inspire them in some way using this passion.

- *Empathy* – Speaking to an audience and being able to understand and/or perceive how they are reacting to your message.

- *Authority* – Speaking about your topic with confidence and in such a way that the audience trusts you and hence sees you as an expert on the topic.

- *Knowledge* – Having the necessary facts and information covering the topic being discussed, over and above the level of knowledge of the average member of the audience.

A person's public speaking persona is built up on how they use and reflect the above characteristics in their regular speaking.

Ways to avoid the temptation to mimic

It is really important that you develop your *own* public speaking persona. As people on the autistic spectrum, one of the ways that we have been able to fit in at school and at work has been to mimic people who we see as being successful.

Frequently, social skills do not come naturally to us, and in order to effectively show these skills to the world, we have made use of our very strong ability to observe details in others, and have effectively copied what they do so that it can appear that we know how to do the correct social things as well. Over time, most of us then learn to adapt this learning to suit us as individuals, but the mimicking served its purpose in the early days to assist us getting through.

When you start speaking publicly, it is very possible that you may start mimicking successful speakers you have heard and seen, especially as you recognise that public speaking is about more than just standing up and talking. In the beginning, as an absolute amateur, it may be necessary to do this to a certain extent, but it is essential that you ultimately try to develop your own unique style.

Part of what makes you unique is understanding exactly what is important to you as a speaker, since this will help define and shape the persona people will see when you step onto the stage and begin to speak.

What is important to me about public speaking is to share my knowledge and insights with other people in such a way as to help them grow as people. For me that's one of the most significant parts of what I want to achieve. I also consider what is important about my message for the people I speak to, and for me it is to show them that I understand where they are coming from and provide inspiration – whether it be to another person on the spectrum, or to someone trying to build their career in the workplace, or an individual trying to overcome what may currently seem to be an insurmountable adversity. Knowing what I want my message to achieve gives me the empathy and passion I need to shape my speaking, and that is part of my persona. It also enabled me to ensure that the persona I was developing as I grew as a speaker was purely mine as opposed to any I may have been inadvertently mimicking.

Now complete Exercise Toolkit 6: Developing Your Speaking Voice (p.168) in Part 5 of the book.

There are a number of elements that make up your speaking persona:

- your personal purpose, as discussed above

- your voice

- your body language and mannerisms, and

- your outward appearance.

Your public speaking voice

As mentioned in Chapter 2, the purpose of this book is not so much to go into the detail of how to speak publicly in general, but rather to examine this from the perspective of our particular strengths and challenges as people on the autistic spectrum.

I am not going to spend time here talking about the perfect public speaking voice and how to make sure you have it. There are a number of excellent books available on developing your voice as a public speaker, and I have given details of two of these in Further Reading. However, for most people on the spectrum, there are four main areas that are worthwhile focusing on when we consider your voice as a public speaker. These are:

- getting your breathing right

- clarity, volume and speed

- the importance of pitch

- important pauses versus hesitation.

Getting your breathing right

If you have never had to speak publicly before, you may be wondering why I am mentioning something so very basic as breathing! Surely the fact that we need to breathe is a *fait accompli*? If, on the other hand, you have had to speak before, you will be aware that it refers not to the act of breathing per se, but rather to how to breathe in the most effective way to support and bolster your voice.

Many people go to make their first speech, only to find that when they start speaking they experience some (or all!) of the following:

- They find that for many sentences they run out of breath for the sentence, having to take a breath in the middle.

- They discover that the audience provides feedback that their voice was far too soft, despite them being convinced their volume was quite high.

- Their voice ends up being trembling or uneven, with volume being inconsistent.

This is the result of not using your breath properly, in the sense of not making correct use of breathing techniques to support your speech. People often make the mistake, when nervous, of tensing their stomachs and not allowing their diaphragm to move enough to fill their lungs sufficiently. As a result, they find that they are suddenly short of breath in a relatively short sentence, and can actually end up feeling breathless. What is happening is that you are breathing quite shallowly rather than breathing deeply. When you are about to start speaking, you want to be able to breathe deeply and fill your lungs with air comfortably, and not struggle throughout your speech with fighting a breathless sensation.

This is quite a specialised area. For this reason, let me refer you to a book called *Voice and Speaking Skills for Dummies* by Judy Apps (2012). Despite the name, this is actually a very useful book when it comes to working through some practical exercises you can do to both become aware of your current use of your breath in speaking, and to develop a more appropriate one. Chapter 4 in particular will walk you through some excellent tools to ensure that you have the right breathing tools for your speaking engagement. I strongly recommend it.

Clarity, volume and speed

Part of ensuring that your speech is clear and logical lies with how you develop your speaking material, as covered in Chapter 10. However, there are some additional considerations.

CLARITY

The first of these is that you need to be aware of how your speaking voice is perceived by others. You need to be aware of qualities that you have, such as a strong accent, difficulty enunciating certain letters, and so forth. Many people on the spectrum and those with other conditions that affect their speech feel that this automatically precludes them from speaking publicly. I absolutely disagree with this, and would encourage you to keep in mind that public speaking can be done by anyone who takes the time to overcome their challenges. Think of Steven Hawking and Stephen Hopson. Both have disabilities that you would assume would make it impossible for them to speak publicly, but both have renowned public speaking careers.

If you are aware that you have a strong accent or difficulty in pronouncing words or sentences, this is something that you should work on. In most cases, this can be addressed by slowing your speech and ensuring that you introduce appropriate pauses. However, if your accent is very strong, you may need to speak to a coach who can help you with this. On the other hand, if you find that you struggle to pronounce certain words clearly, part of addressing this is taking the time to make sure that you enunciate as clearly as you can, without making your speech appear 'robotic' or artificial. Another element that can help is to link your speaking to your body and facial expressions. While this does not always come easily, it can help to make the meaning of a word clear. As a silly example, if you feel that your pronunciation of the word 'whoa' can sometimes sound like the word 'no', using your finger wagging left and right as you say 'no' supports the meaning, whereas putting your hand up in a 'stop' position while you say 'whoa' would clarify that you mean whoa not no.

More than anything, clarity comes from practising. Make sure that if this is a challenge you do experience that you practise frequently – both in front of a mirror and by recording what you say. The recording is useful to play back to others, who can then give you feedback on your voice alone, without seeing any visual aids from you. The mirror can be useful to flag to you if you start overcompensating in your speech through your face, in other words, over-pronouncing words with your mouth, which would be distracting for your audience.

VOLUME

Volume has partially been discussed in the section on the importance of breathing, but there are some important points that still need to be made. The first relates to projecting your voice. When someone asks us to speak up, what they are asking us to do is project our voice so that it can be heard better. What they are not asking you to do is to start shouting. Very often, when we are speaking and we are told we need to speak louder because people at the back cannot hear, we start to shout without realising it. So how do we avoid doing this? Well, there are a couple of things I would recommend to you. First, do take the time to practise speaking out loud before your event. Also, you need to do this in an environment large enough to allow you to project your voice in the first place. For example, if you only practise speaking in front of a mirror, or in front of a friend in your living room, you are going to get used to speaking to people within very close proximity. On the other hand, if you get together with a friend and practise speaking to him as you stand at one end of a tennis court and he stands at the other, this is going to be a very different experience.

The second point to note is how to make your voice project across the hypothetical tennis court above without having to raise your voice into a shout. This comes back to your breathing exercises and how you use your breath. The volume or projection you use in your speech is directly related to the amount of air in your lungs, and how well you can fill them. When you speak to someone in close proximity, you tend to project air out of your lungs using your chest muscles. It isn't important to take deep breaths, since when you are speaking closely, a single breath can last a long time. On the other hand, if you want to project your voice, you need to get more air into your lungs and push it out a little harder than you do when you are speaking to someone closer. Try to visualise that your voice is contained in the airwaves coming from your lungs. When it leaves your mouth it is strong, but as it travels further away from you, it becomes weaker and weaker and starts to dissipate. Therefore, if you are going to speak to people further away from you, you need to ensure that the breath coming from your mouth is strong enough to carry your voice further, as opposed to your voice being louder on the same level of breath.

The way to ensure that you train your body to take in more breath is to focus on using your stomach muscles to pull your diaphragm down, thereby allowing your lungs to inflate further. I am not saying that you have to suck in so much air that you end up pushing out more air than you need. Otherwise you will end up speaking faster than you need to and your speech may end up sounding somewhat like air being released from a balloon! You need to just ensure that you are able to inhale deeply enough to be able to 'push' your voice further when you need to.

As an exercise to see how this works in practice, take a breath and say the word 'speak' once in a long, steady pronunciation for as long as you can before you run out of breath (i.e. say 'speeeeeeeeeeeeeeeeeeeak'). While you are doing this, try to listen to the volume of your voice. Now place the palms of your hands on your stomach with your thumbs just below your ribs. Now repeat the exercise above, taking a breath and saying the word 'speak'. However this time, shortly after starting, press inwards and upwards with your hands as you are saying it. This should have the effect of pushing more air out of your lungs as you speak. You should find that your volume automatically increases as a result. Try this with someone listening if you can, since we sometimes do not notice the difference ourselves but others can. Also note that it is important when doing this exercise that you relax your stomach and lungs to allow this to happen. If you resist pushing the air out, your voice may even become softer.

SPEED

This brings us to speed. One of the greatest temptations when we are standing on the stage going through a pre-rehearsed speech is to get through it as quickly as possible – whether that desire is conscious or subconscious! Because we are familiar with what we are going to say, we tend to go 'full-steam ahead' in our speaking without taking our audience into account. This goes back to the key element of speaking – *empathy*. It is extremely important for you to try to envisage your speech from your audience's perspective. Remember that, although you are familiar with what you are going to say and the key points you are going to make, they are not. You need to ensure that you are speaking at an appropriate speed to allow them to take this in, and you provide sufficient pauses for them to 'digest' what you have just said. I will talk about pauses a little later, but the point here is that you need to ensure you are speaking calmly, smoothly and in a clear, relaxed style – never coming across as rushed or rushing. At the same time, you should make sure that you do not go to the other extreme speaking too slowly, because this can give the audience the impression that you are bored.

The best way to get the balance right is to practise. Time yourself as you say your speech out loud for the first time (or read it if you have written it down), making sure that you leave a one second gap between each sentence. Generally, as we practise and become more familiar with what we intend to say, the time we spend on each sentence becomes shorter and shorter as we begin to subconsciously 'abbreviate' spaces and gaps. Try to make sure that you keep to your original times. Make a note of how long it takes to reach certain key points in the speech, and if you find you are ahead of yourself, pause to take a sip of water, take a breath and start speaking again at a more measured rate.

Keep in mind that when we rush our speaking, our enunciation of words begins to decline, and can make it be more difficult to be understood. Focusing on pronunciation as part of your speech clarity will help you to control your speed as well.

The importance of pitch

When I say pitch, I am talking about the tone and variation you use for your voice as you speak. For most neurotypicals, pitch is an incredibly important part of engagement when it comes to listening to a speaker. If we think of our speaking acronym SPEAK, pitch can be reflected in three elements, *passion* and *charisma*, *empathy* and *authority*. Before I talk about some of the things you should consider in using appropriate pitch for your speech, let us consider some typical types of inappropriate speech.

THE ROBOT

The Robot is someone who drones to the audience in a monotone, using very little or no variation in their tone at all. People run the risk of doing this when they rely too heavily on their notes, since many of us tend to read in a monotone voice. Audiences get extremely bored with this type of speaker, since the speech reflects a lack of passion and authority, and from our perspective it certainly lacks any audience empathy.

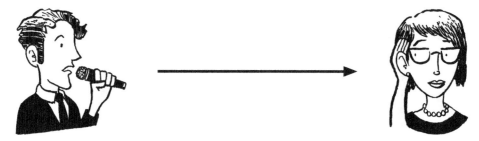

Figure 5.1 Monotone

THE MOORED BOAT IN STORMY WATERS

This is the type of speaker whose pitch goes up and down in regular waves. The trouble with this type of speaking, similar to people sitting in a moored boat on stormy seas, is that people can end up feeling sea-sick. They can get so distracted by the constant up and down that they can end up thinking 'I can't listen to this anymore' and may even leave the room.

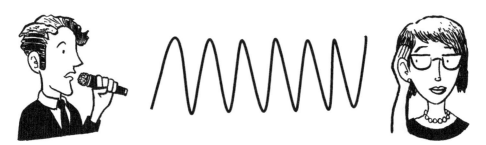

Figure 5.2 Up and down pitch

THE NURSERY TEACHER

The nursery teacher is someone who speaks in a constant high pitch, as if speaking to toddlers or a pet. This can be really tiring for an audience, and can also give the impression that the speaker is being condescending. Speaking to an audience as if they are children can give offence…

Figure 5.3 High pitch tone

THE SHOCK THERAPIST

The shock therapist is someone who speaks at a neutral pitch, only to suddenly increase both the pitch and volume at which they are speaking in a dramatic fashion, and does this regularly throughout their speech. Equate this to watching a horror movie where the music is gentle or quiet, only for you to leap out of your seat as the music suddenly blasts out dramatically as a climax is reached. If this style is a part of your speech that you are deliberately inserting into your presentation mix, this is fine, but a 'shock therapist' is someone who speaks like this all the time without realising it. They tend to startle and alarm the audience rather than engaging them.

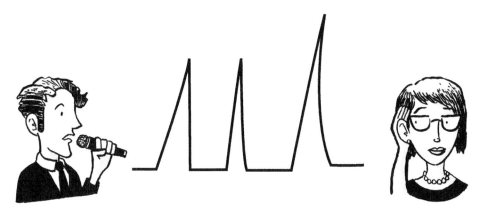

Figure 5.4 Sudden increase(s) in pitch and tone

The best description for the type of pitch you should be using in your speaking is that of a story-teller. If you are listening to someone telling you a story – either directly or by means of an audiobook or the radio – you tend to get engrossed in the tale due to the way that the person tells it. If you have time, find either a recording of a person telling a story or get a good story-teller to read you something. You will notice that their pitch and tone will vary, not in the regular 'up/down' way the moored boat in stormy waters does, but relative to the story they are telling. Perhaps the most important element of this is that they are reflecting their passion in their reading. If it is a particularly important point they are making, then you will hear them emphasise this, using volume and pitch to draw your attention to it. This is how you should aim to speak.

Important pauses versus hesitation

One of the important distinctions that you will need to learn to make is the distinction between an appropriate pause and a hesitation. When we think about pauses in our speaking, these tend to be associated with such things as a change in emphasis or the start of a new section. In fact, pauses can be used for some additional purposes to very good effect. For example, if you are telling people something that they are eager to hear the resolution or conclusion of, a pause just before announcing that conclusion can have the effect of making people focus their attention that much more, or lean forward in anticipation. Similarly, if you have just made a particular point that you want people to reflect on momentarily, this is a good time to interject a pause while keeping eye contact with your audience.

On the other hand, hesitation is where there is a pause in your speech with no apparent reason, or one that appears to be longer than necessary. These should be avoided, since they can result in the audience becoming frustrated or uncomfortable. They also run the risk of being interpreted as gap-fillers.

A gap-filler is an unnecessary or unwanted word or phrase that can end up being repeated during a speech and distracting your audience. Examples of gap-fillers are words and phrases like 'um', 'anyway', 'so anyway', 'as I was saying' and so on. The filler 'um' is one of the most notorious words when it comes to speaking, and the worst thing about it is that most of the time we don't even realise we are using it. Do a test for yourself. Get someone to record you speaking for half an hour. Afterwards, watch the recording and count just how many 'um's you have used, or how many other gap-fillers you have used. You may find it quite surprising, especially if this isn't something you have considered before.

The most important part of developing your public speaking persona is to recognise that this is how you represent yourself to the public. It is extremely rare for a public speaker to present his or her entire personality to an audience as part of their persona. This is not any type of misrepresentation of who you are, but rather a filtering of who you are. You as an individual have many unique and valuable elements, but it is for you to decide what parts of that character you want to show to the public.

Some people find it useful to define their public speaking personality as completely separate from themselves. So, for example, some people say that they define themselves by the character they reflect, such as the joker or the adventurer. While I think this may be useful for some people, I do not believe this is useful for everyone. I see this as far more artificial than just 'filtering' my character for the purposes of a public speaking persona. However, this can be a powerful tool for some people who struggle to present themselves on the stage for whatever reason. I suggest that if you feel this is something that could work for you, you investigate it and try it out. Get feedback from others as to how it is working for you, and how you are appearing to the audience.

Chapter 6

Acknowledging Others

When speaking on behalf of our organisations or speaking on a cause of particular interest to us, our focus tends to be on what we are saying and the message we are trying to share with the audience. We will spend much of our time focusing on the key elements to be communicated and, as you will learn as you progress through this book, some of the subtleties of how to make the message memorable. All of this is, of course, absolutely essential for you as a public speaker.

However, it is also very important to acknowledge others.

What do I mean by acknowledging others?

When we are speaking about something that is particularly important for our company or for a cause we are supporting, one of the most important ways to ensure we have the ongoing support and input from anyone who has been involved in making that event successful is to publicly acknowledge their effort. It is human nature for us to want to be acknowledged if we have made an effort to help support something or someone, especially if:

1. this has taken a lot of effort on our part

2. we have made personal sacrifices in order to help out, and/or

3. the event has been a significant success.

Being acknowledged makes us feel that we are indeed part of the success of whatever has happened, and that our efforts have not just been invisible or in the background.

The Asperger challenge

As a person on the autistic spectrum, some of us experience a challenge when it comes to the area of what is called empathy. Tony Attwood (2007) says of this that children with Asperger's tend to be immature when it comes to managing emotions and that we struggle to express empathy (2007). He also states that we frequently compensate for this by mimicking other people, effectively becoming quite accurate 'actors' when it comes to the outward display of how we should act, without necessarily having the insight. As a result, when we become adults people may not easily see that we struggle with empathy since we have perfected the art of mimicking others. Temple Grandin also acknowledges that this can be a challenge in her book *Thinking in Pictures* (Grandin 2006). Like many of us, Temple had to learn to empathise with people, rather than this being something that came naturally. Now, I do not believe that those of us on the spectrum cannot experience empathy. I actually believe that we experience it very strongly as a whole, but have learnt to 'block it off' as a coping mechanism. Many of us are able to very accurately identify when there is a change in atmosphere in a room, for example, without being able to identify exactly why these changes occur or what they mean. So if we think about being able to empathise with people, often we may pick up that 'there is something wrong' without being able to recognise just what that is.

Coming from this perspective, then, many of us may just not notice if the people we work with are feeling upset in any way because we did not acknowledge their contributions at an appropriate time. When we pull together a speech or presentation, we are generally thinking about the technical content of that speech and how we can get our message across optimally. It tends not to come as second nature for us to build acknowledgements into our speech. After all, what does that have to do the technical area we are talking about?

However, as mentioned above, it is considered really important in delivering speeches that we do actually build in acknowledgements where appropriate, without over-acknowledging every possible person who has been involved in the area we are speaking about.

How do I know who to acknowledge?

Before I go on to talk about the best ways to acknowledge people in your speech, let's just give a thought to who it is appropriate to be acknowledging in the first place.

Frequently, those of us with Asperger syndrome or ASD tend to imagine that we are providing sufficient recognition to those in our companies and teams just by representing them – after all, if they weren't doing a good job, you wouldn't be there. However, if you analyse the speeches of a lot of us who have not particularly considered acknowledging others, in all likelihood you find a lot of references to 'the company', and 'I'. Let's expand our speech to include more 'our' and 'we' references.

If you are representing your company to speak about some key event that has taken place within the company, this is a particularly important time to acknowledge those people in your company and team who have helped make this a success. In most cases almost all of the people in your company or department have contributed to the success of the event, and it is perfectly acceptable to do your acknowledgements at this top level. I will speak about how you can build this into your speech later in the chapter.

One thing you need to avoid is being too specific about who you acknowledge. Let me explain what I mean by this with a hypothetical case study.

Case study: Under- and over-acknowledging people at HCS

Cassandra Wells was Director of Corporate Services at a medium-sized company called HCS. Over the last 18 months the organisation had been going through a complete restructuring of its infrastructure, not only in terms of IT but also with respect to office layouts, organisational design and cost centres. The restructure had been achieved below budget and well within project timescales and since implementation there had been extremely positive feedback. In fact, the restructure had resulted in a reduction in overheads of over 20 per cent in the last quarter – a significant cost saving for the company.

Cassandra was delighted to receive an invitation to discuss the success of the restructure at a national conference on realigning corporate services to the business strategy. The event was a very high profile one, and being invited to be a speaker there was seen by Cassandra as the final validation of all her hard work.

In pulling together her speech, Cassandra had been advised by her colleagues on the Board that it was important to remember to acknowledge the contribution of staff. Personally, she was pleased to have the advice, since she would never have thought of building that into her speech had the comment not been made. She took the advice she was given and made sure that she added what she felt were appropriate acknowledgements at salient points in her speech.

The day of her speech came and Cassandra did her best to give a strong, confident and engaging speech to her audience. She made sure that she acknowledged the five people in the company whom she felt had made a significant contribution to the success of the programme, as well as the finance team in the company as a whole. At the end she had what she felt was a very positive response, and the post-speech networking reinforced her initial perception.

When she returned to work the following week, she was even more pleased to hear that the conference had been recorded, and that her speech had been uploaded to the company intranet for all staff to watch. She was pleased that people would have a chance to see that she had noted their input, because she really did value their contributions, even if she didn't perhaps say so as frequently as she should.

However, as time went on, certain people in the organisation appeared to be less friendly and supportive than they had been before the conference. At first Cassandra thought she may be imagining the change. After all, she wasn't all that good at understanding people or being able to interpret moods. But her concern appeared to have substance. People who would have stopped to speak with her in the corridor or have a chat with her in the canteen now walked past her without appearing to notice her, or even giving her a sort of 'down your nose' look before walking away. Still others seemed to be angry with her for some reason. Confused, Cassandra went to speak to one of her colleagues, Roland, whom she had trusted with the knowledge of her diagnosis of ASD, and who she was able to speak with for some frank answers.

'Roland,' she said on reaching his office, 'I really don't know what's going on. I don't know if I am imagining this or not, but something seems to be wrong with my communication with staff…'

Roland smiled at her with one of those smiles that made Cassandra wonder if he was happy for her, embarrassed for her or showing sympathy towards her.

'You really don't know, do you?' he asked.

'Know what?'

Roland sighed.

'You know you said Michael advised you to acknowledge the staff contribution…?'

'Yeah – and I did!'

Roland nodded, rubbing his chin.

'Yes you did – but you made a big deal of really acknowledging some people, while not even mentioning others…'

Cassandra frowned.

'That's not true. Sure, I mentioned the key people. But then I said a general thanks to everyone else.'

> Roland smiled again, this time nodding passionately.
>
> 'Exactly, Cassandra! And therein lies the problem. Your speech upset a lot of people because of who you acknowledged...'
>
> Cassandra jumped to her feet, waving her hands around in frustration.
>
> 'I don't get it! I just don't get it!! First I'm being told my speech is wrong because I don't acknowledge people, now I am told my speech was wrong *because* I acknowledged people! How on earth am I ever supposed to know what to do?'

I think a lot of people reading the above example could be nodding in agreement with Cassandra and asking exactly the same question she did – how am I ever supposed to know what to do? Well, let me start to answer that by asking you whether or not you were able to identify what was happening in Cassandra's company and why? Don't be surprised if you answer 'no'. For those of us on the autistic spectrum, office politics is a very challenging topic.

Let's consider what actually happened with Cassandra's speech. We note that Cassandra did in fact acknowledge five particular people, as well as the finance team. Therefore, acknowledgements were indeed made. However, what Cassandra had inadvertently done by very specifically mentioning five people and one team was to exclude anyone else's contribution and make them feel that their input was less important than those people she mentioned. A side-effect in the office was that people ended up being resentful of the individuals who were seen as being praised by her in the conference, and they ended up having a lot of negative feedback from their colleagues at work and were treated as the 'manager's pets' even though that wasn't actually what the situation was. Similarly, the fact that the finance team was the only department to receive an acknowledgement ended up alienating the finance team from the rest of corporate services, a very uncomfortable situation for them.

As a result of this, the majority of people ended up feeling resentful of Cassandra – either because they felt under-appreciated, or because they felt that she had created tensions in the workplace for them.

This is an example of over-acknowledging people in your speech.

So what is the best way to acknowledge people in your business? In general, the best way is to make a general acknowledgement, such as 'This programme of work would not have been the success it is without the dedication and hard work of the people at HCS...' Where there are one or two individuals in particular who do warrant a particular mention, such as a programme manager or project manager, then it is best to acknowledge them together with others. For example, 'A special mention does need to be extended to Martin Henry, the project manager for this piece of work, who – *together with the project team* – helped us to complete the project within budget…'

If you are speaking on behalf of a cause or some sort of fund raising activity, it is really important to ensure that you do acknowledge those supporters who have helped in your success by pledging money, and those who have volunteered time. Now, it is not possible to mention every single person who has helped to make something successful. Think of a charity reaching its donation goal. It is highly likely that there have been several hundred (if not thousand!) people involved in this achievement. You cannot possibly acknowledge everyone individually, but you certainly can acknowledge them as a group. So make sure that in this sort of situation you acknowledge (a) your supporters who have pledged money, (b) your supporters who have volunteered their time to support you, and (c) your employees and peers. It is also generally important to acknowledge them in that order.

Now that we have spoken about how to acknowledge others in your speech, let's start to think about what you can do to make your speech memorable for your audience by developing and using key elements of your own unique speaking persona.

Chapter 7

How do Inspirational Speakers Succeed?

In my opinion, one of the best compliments a public speaker can receive is to be referred to as a charismatic speaker. Let me clarify why I feel that this is such an important element of public speaking.

Speaking with charisma – just what is that?

The Oxford Dictionary of English (2010) definition of charisma reads: 'a compelling attractiveness or charm that can inspire devotion in others'. The Collins Concise English Dictionary (2013) adds to this by referring to charisma as 'a special power that some people have naturally that makes them able to influence other people and attract their attention and admiration.'

I would adapt this latter definition slightly to give a more appropriate definition of charisma from the perspective of public speaking by adding '...and frequently inspiring people coming into contact with them'. A charismatic speaker is someone who captivates his or her audience, and inspires them in some way or another. From my perspective, this should be about inspiring them to achieve something personally, although frequently the inspiration can centre on the public figure (such as being inspired to read all their books and follow any blogs and social media sites they have). I believe that if you are not inspiring people to do something for themselves personally, you are not achieving all you are capable of. After all, I believe this is the reason most of us are speaking publicly.

When I read the descriptions of charisma given above once more, however, there is one particular part that I do not agree with. This relates to the statement that people who are charismatic have this naturally. I would argue that charisma, like any other business skill, is something that can be developed in anyone, provided you know what it is that makes a person appear charismatic as well as what it is about yourself that makes you unique.

I would also argue against what many psychologists believe to be the source of charisma. According to a number of psychologists, charisma is built upon an individual's ability to express and control their emotions, as well as to be sensitive to the emotions of others. They also highlight social expressiveness and sensitivity as being key criteria as well. Needless to say, for most of us on the autistic spectrum, this would mean that we would stand little chance of ever being charismatic, since social and emotional sensitivity tend not to be our natural strengths. However, despite that there are a number of people who would certainly classify as being charismatic who are on the autistic spectrum, such as Temple Grandin and Michael John Carley.

I therefore believe that charisma is something that we can develop in the same way that many of us have learnt to develop our interaction and teamwork skills for the workplace.

Let us concentrate on the most important considerations to ensure that you are moving in the right direction towards charismatic speaking.

What are the core elements of personal charisma?

There are three main components of charisma, namely influence, presence and benevolence. If we think about our key elements of public speaking, namely SPEAK, we can relate these components as follows:

Influence

When I speak about influence here, I am talking about the perception of the audience that the person concerned has something very special to offer, either due to their special knowledge, position in a business or sector, high intellect or even high financial value. In terms of SPEAK, this would equate to your *authority* and *knowledge* elements.

Benevolence

By benevolence, I mean that the person has an interest in the welfare or concerns of others. Think about some people who have been very influential for you. In general, it is relatively unusual for you to see people who do not appear to have any interest in others as charismatic. Part of the attractiveness of the individual is the fact that they want to use their influence to benefit others, rather than purely for their own benefit. As far as SPEAK goes, we are looking here at the elements of *empathy* – understanding and acknowledging the needs of others – and *passion*, namely how strongly you are able to show your interest in the area concerned (for the benefit of others).

Presence

This component is less directly represented in SPEAK, but let me clarify that by explaining what I mean by presence. We say that someone has presence when their influence is felt in a place without their having to say anything. Now, this is potentially an area that many people, both neurotypical and those with ASD, may experience as confusing. How can someone influence a meeting just by being there and not saying anything? The reason this is not so easily understood by many of us is that this is very much an expression of your body language – something many people (both on and off the autistic spectrum) do not have full insight into.

People who are said to have presence are considered to be people who are completely committed to the meeting at hand, completely present and completely attentive. The way people pick this attentiveness up is by means of body language and subtle facial and bodily cues. This is quite a detailed topic that I will be covering in another book, but the important point to make here is that this is very closely linked to your self-awareness as a first step (our S in SPEAK). In order for you to be able to project to others that you are present and attentive, you need to be aware of the signals you are currently projecting through your body language. Some of the key things which may negate this is if you are tense, worried or in any way either physically or mentally uncomfortable. No matter how much you may try to hide this, it will end up being reflected in your subconscious body language to some extent.

Having detailed the three components of charisma, let us consider how best to optimise these in our speaking. I would say that for most of us, the areas we tend to be stronger in terms of these components are those of influence and benevolence. That is not to say that we are not going to be strong in presence, but this may be a component we need to review so that we learn how to project our better body language.

As far as influence goes, we can be seen as influential due to our special levels of knowledge of key areas, our unique insights, our unique experiences. For some of us, we also have particularly high levels of academic qualifications, recognisable indicators of intellectual skills. Other areas of influence include a history of success – for example, as a successful business person, a successful fundraiser, and so forth. These are the sorts of indicators of success that audiences are drawn to as far as public speaking goes.

We tend to be stronger in the area of benevolence due to the fact that most of us are very passionate about what we speak about. Even if we feel that we generally don't do that brilliant a job of reflecting our emotions in general,

I can assure you that when you feel passionate about something, it is highly unlikely that the energy and commitment linked to that can be hidden.

What else can we do to ensure that our speeches are memorable?

Speaking is not just about presenting a set of facts to a captive audience. Public speaking is about making an impression to an audience with the result that they leave the venue thinking about what you have said, and that that they ultimately share positively the message you gave to them. If you undertake a speaking engagement and people provide feedback after your speech along the lines of 'Hmm. Very interesting.' or 'Some interesting facts.' and yet follow-up three months later shows most people have forgotten you, then you know you have not done a good job as far as your actual presentation goes.

We need to ensure that we capture and keep the attention of our audience. As well as ensuring that the material you present is appropriate and addresses the needs if the audience, you also need to make sure that you present it in a way that makes people enjoy listening to you. One of the best ways to do this is to introduce a little bit of laughter or emotional energy.

Introducing laughter

In some ways, introducing laughter can be something that is easier for us to achieve. All that we need to do is ensure that we are inserting 'smile points' at appropriate times in our speech, and that the 'smile points' are the result of comments or jokes that flow with the speech itself. For example, if we are speaking about the challenges of disabilities in the workplace, an example used in the speech could be about the challenge a manager may experience on interviewing an amputee without a right arm – how do they shake their hand? An appropriate 'smile point' could be to do a visual of what the manager may do (in other words, 'play act' the scene, showing the manager standing up, offering his hand, saying 'oops', pulling his hand back, hesitating, etc). This would be seen as appropriate joke because it is highlighting an actual problem in a humorous way without being offensive. On the other hand, interjecting a joke just because it is funny, irrespective of whether it flows with what you are talking about is just going to confuse the audience – why did he/she say that? That's a weird deviation from what he/she was speaking about! Another consideration is your topic. Some topics are just not conducive to jokes at any time. Make sure you use your judgment on this point and if you are not sure, ask someone you trust.

Introducing visuals

The use of visuals can be a very important way to ensure that the message you give is remembered after the event. I have spoken about this in a lot more detail in Chapter 10, but suffice to say that if you are going to use slides or other visuals, make sure that they are really impactful. A visual in the form of a slide can say so much more to an audience that you can alone. If your slides look amateurish or plain, this will completely override any professional image you may have presented due to your speaking or personal presentation. On the other hand, a powerful, sophisticated or highly impactful slide will make your audience sit back and think, 'Wow! This guy knows his stuff!'

Producing handouts

Like visuals on the screen, handouts can also make a powerful impression and be useful for later application by the audience. However, make sure that you do not hand these out ahead of or during your speech, or they will end up detracting from your presentation. Hand them out afterwards.

Let me end the chapter by emphasising that inspirational speaking is less about a technique and more about your personal energy and passion. Audiences are always attracted to people who can reflect their energy, passion and enthusiasm for their topic. Make sure that you do not feel that you cannot share your passion with them. After all, that is probably a large part of why you are speaking in the first place!

Before you continue your reading, refer back to Toolkit Exercise 2: Key Elements of Public Speaking (p.151) in Part 5 of the book. Take the time now to complete the same questions, but taking into account any additional insights you may have gained during your reading to date. Where you feel your insights have changed, enter these in the Point 1 row.

PART 3

Preparing for a Public Speaking Engagement

Chapter 8

Researching Your Audience

When we are preparing for a speech, the main activities that most people consider are what they need to do to prepare themselves (as we have been discussing so far) and what they need to do to make the speech itself engaging and interesting. While both of those areas are critically important (and will be covered in the next couple of chapters), there are two further activities that should be undertaken to properly prepare for a speaking engagement, both of which are particularly important for those of us on the autistic spectrum. The first of these is to research the audience you will be speaking to, and the second is to research the venue you will be presenting at. The latter is covered in Chapter 12, but researching your audience is something that a potential public speaker needs to do before he or she starts to prepare any material, or think about how they will present themselves. For this reason, I am going to speak about this topic first.

Why is it important to understand your audience?

In Chapter 3 we spoke about types of public speaking and how the requirements and expectations of people attending events can differ significantly. As a speaker, it is important for you to understand the various types of audience and how this can affect both how you deliver your speech and the material you present. Recognising the visual clues and body language from the audience tends to be more challenging for those of us with an autistic spectrum disorder, and therefore it is important that we do as much as we can beforehand to ensure that what we present is appropriate to the particular audience concerned, since we may miss visual cues during our speech.

Let me elaborate with an example.

Case study: Developing a speech for the wrong audience

Patrick Emmit had received an invitation to give a speech on the topic of autism and dyslexia, a topic that he had been discussing in a number of forums and online panels. Determined to make a good impression, he prepared his speech to incorporate the latest statistics on the link between autism and dyslexia, and ensured that he had sufficient references to international research on the topic.

On reaching the venue, he set up his overhead projector and waited for the audience to arrive. The organiser came and thanked him for taking part and said that she was certain his presentation would help a lot of people. At that point the audience arrived. Patrick was completely surprised to see that his audience comprised a group of school children and their parents. Heart pounding, he quickly looked around for anything that would describe what he was presenting. Finding a leaflet, he quickly read it, and felt his heart drop. The purpose of the speaking engagement was to present to high school children with high functioning autism and dyslexia on how best to develop coping strategies, and to use his own life as an example of how you can achieve a successful career despite these conditions. Patrick's speech had been aimed at a senior practitioner or academic audience, since he was under the impression that he was speaking to psychologists and researchers in the area of autism and/or dyslexia. What a total disaster!

The above example emphasises just how important it is to know exactly what audience you are presenting to when you prepare your speech. If Patrick had known that what he was actually being asked to do was undertake a motivational speech to youngsters and their families, his approach would have been totally different, and he would not have spent all his time focused on making his speech as 'professional' and academic as possible.

So let us briefly consider what the various types of audience are and their expectations.

What are the various types of audience and what do they expect?

Let us consider again the types of speech that were introduced in Chapter 3. The main types of public speaking are:

- speaking on behalf of yourself as a specialist or professional

- academic speaking

- internal presentations to your team

- internal presentations to your company

- speaking on behalf of your company at a public event.

So what are the types of audience that can be associated with each of these speaking engagements? Probably the easiest one to consider is that of *academic speaking*. When you speak, your audience is going to be expecting to hear information of a highly academic and rigorous nature. They will not be surprised to be presented with the kinds of facts, figures and statistics Patrick had pulled together as part of his presentation. In fact, if these were missing, the speech would in all likelihood be seen as less authoritative.

Next, let's look at an audience that consist of *people from your company*. There are two scenarios given above for presenting internally at your company, but in general your audience can be considered relatively similar (although if you think about wording and style, for example, there will be subtle differences between the two).

A speech *on behalf of your company* could be to a few different types of audience – are they investors, the media, beneficiaries?

On the other hand, if you are speaking on behalf of yourself *as a specialist or professional*, your audience can vary considerably. You could be speaking to an academic audience, or an audience of people similar to yourself whom you are providing a motivational talk to, or you could be presenting to people with a professional interest in the topic, or people with some other personal interest in the topic (e.g. parents of the children in the examples above). Which type of audience can greatly influence what your speech looks like and the way in which you present it, because each one has its own set of expectations and needs. To make sure that you can pull together the most effective and successful presentation for the audience concerned, you need to understand your audience.

We have said previously that the key elements of successful public speaking centre around SPEAK – self-knowledge, passion and charisma, empathy, authority and knowledge. Being able to understand what your audience wants and is hoping to hear from you is a key part of *empathy*, while knowing how you personally are able to fill this need is part of your *self-knowledge*. Pulling together your knowledge of your audience and your knowledge of yourself in such a way that the speech you develop will engage your audience, fulfil those expectations and inspire them is part of *passion and charisma*.

How to research your audience

So you now know that you need to research your audience before you start developing your speech in detail. How exactly do you go about doing this? There are a few simple steps that will help you find out all you need to know in order to ensure your speech is focused on the right type of audience.

1. *Research the person or organisation that invited you* – Do an internet search of the person or the organisation that invited you to speak. This can provide you with some valuable insights into the type of events they normally host. For example, if you find that the company hosting the event is one that hosts a lot of corporate events, it is very likely that you would have a business audience. On the other hand, if the company or person who invited you generally hosts academic events, you are likely to find yourself presenting to a group of academics.

2. *Research the event and venue* – Try to find out some more about the event in particular, as well as the venue it is being held at. It is important to research the venue, because it may give you some clues about dress-code (if this is not explicit in the invitation). For example, being invited to speak at a formal black-tie award ceremony is very different to being invited to speak to a high school to motivate youngsters. In addition, if this event has any sort of internet advertising or other media announcements, the tone of these will generally make it clear what audience is being targeted. Another thing about the event publicity and the venue is that this may give you a clearer picture of the potential size of the audience. If the event is being held in a small seminar room, you know that your audience is likely to be small, and the format will be less formal. There is the possibility that questions could be asked during your speech, and you may want to build into your introduction that you either welcome questions, or that you welcome questions but ask that they are kept until the end of the speech. On the other hand, if the venue is being held in a stadium-sized conference venue, you know that there will be a large number of people and informal questions or comments are unlikely.

3. *Research other speakers at the event* – If you have access to the details of other people speaking at the same event, try to get some publicly available information on them. Look them up on the social media sites, or do a search for them on the internet. This will help you be aware of who else is attending, and also be a bit knowledgeable about the sorts of speaking these people usually undertake – if any.

4. *If in any doubt, ask your host* – Many people feel embarrassed to ask their hosts for specific information such as exactly who the audience is for an event. However, you certainly shouldn't feel concerned to do this. It is a regular activity undertaken by many people, autistic or neurotypical, and certainly is not a sign of lack of knowledge or ignorance on your side. If you have done your own research and are still not comfortable about the type of presentation your should pull together, contact your host directly and ask them to confirm who the audience of the event is likely to be. Anyone who has hosted an event before will be expecting this question and will be able to answer it.

Making sure your presentation is pitched toward that audience

Now that you know the type of audience you will be presenting to, you need to think about the most appropriate way to engage that particular type of audience. This goes back to what I was speaking about earlier in the chapter, as well as what was covered in Chapter 3. You need to develop your materials and speaking style to be optimal for that particular audience. For example, speaking to other people on the spectrum is very different to speaking to neurotypicals and therapists. Are you speaking to adults or children? Laymen or academics? Experts in your area or novices?

If you are not sure what sort of style works with a particular type of audience, it is always useful to see if you can research a previous speech to a similar audience. The ideal in this respect is to attend a conference or event with a similar 'audience-theme', although in this electronic age you can also find a lot of presentations on the internet on sites such as TEDtalks, and so forth.

Most important of all, make sure that you develop your speech around your own unique speaking persona, albeit directed towards a particular audience's needs and expectations. Avoid that ever-present temptation to mimic what you see others do when they are speaking to similar audiences. You are looking at how you can adapt your unique style if appropriate, not how to take on someone else's.

Chapter 9

Researching Your Topic

When it comes to having information about a topic that is of particular interest to us, people on the autistic spectrum tend to have an advantage over neurotypicals. We tend to have voluminous amounts of data in our heads about the topic in question, because if something interests us we tend to find out as much about it as we possibly can. While this may be a great advantage for us as a whole if we are specialists in the field concerned, it isn't necessarily an advantage when it comes to preparing to speak about that particular topic. After all, if we have such a huge amount of information to share, how do we effectively decide what to share in the restricted timeframe of a speech, and just how should that selected information be presented? This is where researching your topic comes in.

On the other hand, if you are being asked to undertake a speaking engagement on behalf of your company on a topic that is not particularly of interest to you, you will need to gather pertinent information, since it is highly unlikely that you will immediately have that information to hand. In this scenario, you are researching your topic, not only considering how best to present it.

The above two scenarios are very different, and for this reason I cover them separately in the rest of the chapter. I will initially consider the situation in which most of us are likely to speak, where we are asked to speak on a topic of particular interest to us, or on our area of specialism. I will follow that by examining how best to handle the situation where you have to speak on a topic that you are not that familiar with.

Applying SPEAK to speaking on a topic of interest

Let us think again about the key elements for success in public speaking, namely the elements of SPEAK, and consider how these apply to our discussion. I list these here in order of relevance to the discussion.

Self-knowledge

You need to be aware of the fact that, as an individual with ASD, if you are speaking on a topic that you have a particular interest in, it is highly likely (as outlined above) that you will have more information than you can possibly hope to share in a single public speaking event. You should also be aware that you will want to share as much information as you can.

Passion and charisma

If you are speaking about a topic of particular interest to you, there will be no question of you having a passion for it. This is highly likely to come out in your presentation skills and for this reason I will not be discussing this any further here.

Knowledge

As mentioned in the opening of the chapter, knowledge is something you will no doubt have in significant amounts. The challenge for you is deciding just how much of that knowledge is relevant and how it should be shared. Knowing how you handle information relating to a topic of interest is very important in researching how best to present it to your audience.

Authority

Many people assume that if they are speaking in a specialist area or on a topic of particular interest, they will automatically come across as an authority on the subject. In fact, this is not an automatic correlation. In order to come across as an authority on the topic, you need to present yourself confidently and also present your information in a way that meets the needs and expectations of your audience.

Empathy

This element is an extremely important consideration in this situation. In order to pull together a speech that is not only going to share the information you want to share, but also meet the expectations of the audience, it is essential that you take the time to try to understand exactly what it is that the audience is expecting from you. This means trying to see things through their eyes – generally more of a challenge for those of us on the autistic spectrum.

If we summarise the most important points, we can see that in considering what to share when speaking on a topic of particular interest, there are three really important things we need to take into account:

- We need to consider just how much information to share that is relevant.

- We need to consider what the audience is expecting to hear.

- We need to consider how we can best present that relevant information to meet those audience needs and expectations – and potentially surpass them.

Determining how much information is relevant

The first step to take in narrowing down your available information is to consider exactly what is relevant to that audience on that day. What do I mean by this? Your area of speciality or interest may be particularly broad, and it is highly unlikely that any single speaking event is going to cover every nuance of it. You will therefore need to research which aspect of the topic you are speaking about is relevant to the conference or event you are attending. Let me give you an example to clarify.

If I go to a conference to speak on the topic of change management, it is essential I trim down my knowledge bank ahead of considering what information to include in my speech, since change management is an extremely broad and extensive topic. I need to determine the audience (as we have discussed in Chapter 8) by considering such things as whether they are international or national, whether they are academics, business people or lay-people, whether they are specialists or generalists, and so on. Next, I would consider the nature of the conference – is the focus of the conference on the theory of change management? The history of change management? New concepts in change management? A mixture of those? Or is it a practical conference on how people can undertake change management programmes in their organisations? Or is it to review some of the change management programmes I have undertaken?

As you can see from this example, there are various different interpretations of the information that potentially need to be taken into account in deciding what information to include. In general, the nature of the conference is the most valuable determinant of what sort of information you should include, followed by the type of audience you are presenting to.

Once you have that information, you can start to think about how much information to include so that you can comfortably present a speech in the time allocation you have. You need to make sure that you are not putting so much information into your speech so that you end up rushing it, or so little that the speech appears vague or too high-level. The best approach for a public speaker is generally to have less information covered in more detail rather than lots of information covered briefly, since that can give the impression that you do not really know your stuff.

Determining what the audience is expecting to hear

Determining exactly what the audience is expecting or anticipating hearing as part of your speech requires you to make use of that very challenging success factor for public speaking – empathy. I recognise that for the majority of us, empathising with others is not a natural process and therefore can be challenging. However, I totally believe that this is something we can learn to do, albeit to varying degrees depending on the situation and the people involved.

Before you can try to decide what information is relevant for your audience, the first step is to understand your audience. You should have undertaken this as part of your exercise to research your audience, as covered in Chapter 8. However, if you have not done this, I recommend that you do this exercise before you try to determine how best to present your topic.

Once you have completed the exercise in Chapter 8, you will have a good idea of the *type* of audience you will be presenting to and the format they would expecting your presentation to take. Now let us think about what we need to consider in general.

If we think about the topic we are going to speak about, most of us have a tendency to consider what it is about the topic that *we* find interesting as opposed to thinking about what it is that other people may find interesting about the topic. This is a general tendency for most people, including neurotypicals. The difference is that when a neurotypical is reminded or advised to consider the audience, they generally have no difficulties doing so, whereas this can be quite challenging for us.

One technique that I tend to use to help me do this may be of value to you as well. When I have ascertained the nature of the audience I am presenting to as well as the type of information I am likely to be sharing, I then do the following. I try to imagine that I am attending a conference to hear about something that I am interested in hearing about, but do not know much, if anything, about – (the level of my knowledge would be in line with the nature of the audience I am presenting to). I then ask myself the following questions:

- Not knowing that much about the topic, what would I expect the speaker to be sharing with me?

- What particular information would be most valuable for me?

- What sort of format would be most useful for me to understand and remember the details of this new area?

- What sort of information would I *not* want to hear about if this isn't an area that I specialise in?

Using this as a starting point, I look at my shortened information list and decide what I should consider including and what would fall into the 'what they wouldn't want to hear about' category.

So let us apply that to an example. I have been asked to speak at a conference on the topic of autism in the workplace. I have researched the audience, and they are predominantly human resources and health and safety executives. As a result, I have shortened my 'information bank' to be restricted to details concerning employing people with autism, their contribution in the workplace, how to make the environment more autism-friendly, and explaining about and dealing with sensory overloads. I exclude my knowledge about how people on the spectrum can do better in the workplace, how they can handle overload issues in the workplace, and any other areas that are more suited to an audience of people on the spectrum.

Next imagine that I have been invited to attend a conference on diabetes in the workplace because I need to know about this as CEO of a consultancy. I then ask myself the following questions:

- Not knowing that much about the topic, what would I expect the speaker to be sharing with me? I would want to understand how prevalent diabetes is, what are my responsibilities as an employer, what are the key symptoms and what should we do if someone falls ill. I would also want to know if the person with diabetes would want us to do anything in the workplace to help them.

- What particular information would be most valuable for me? What are my responsibilities? What is best practice?

- What sort of format would be most useful for me to understand and remember the details of this new area?

- What sort of information would I *not* want to hear about if this isn't an area that I specialise in? Too much information about the history of diabetes, who it affects and how to avoid developing it. I really wouldn't be that interested in statistics other than overall prevalence.

I would then apply the above answers to consider my autism in the workplace speech inclusion criteria.

What I have effectively done in the example above is applied the criteria of empathy towards the audience, but indirectly. I have not asked 'What will the audience want?' I have asked the indirect question 'What would I want if I was a member of the audience covering a slightly different topic?' and then applied the results of this shift in perspective back to the direct question. I have found this method extremely useful in overcoming challenges I have experienced in trying to empathise with others in this area. What we are effectively doing here is using a variant of the technique of 'putting ourselves in other people's shoes'. When we put ourselves in someone else's shoes, we try to imagine how they are feeling and what they would do. In my technique we are actually trying to imagine what *we* would do in a similar situation, and then projecting that to the other person. I would say that what we are doing is 'putting ourselves in our own shoes but in someone else's situation'. Similar, but subtly different!

Applying SPEAK to speaking on a non-specialist topic

Now that we have considered what we would do to 'trim down' what we would present to our audiences if we are talking about one of our areas of special interest, we should consider the situation of being asked to speak on a topic that is not a particular area of interest for us. Let us think again about the key elements for success in public speaking, namely the elements of SPEAK, and how these apply to our discussion. Again, I list these here in order of relevance to the discussion.

Self-knowledge

You need to be aware of the fact that, as an individual with ASD, if you are speaking on a topic that you do not have a particular interest in, it is highly likely that when you start researching the topic, you will research it in too much detail, because we do like to gather as much information on a topic as we can. Part of our challenge then, is to be very specific about just how much information you should be gathering, given the time constraints and the nature of the speaking event.

Passion and charisma

Unlike speaking about a topic of particular interest, there is no guarantee that when you speak about your topic that it will come across with passion or charisma. Therefore, it is important that you consider your speaking style more in this type of speech than you would in one where you are intrinsically passionate.

Knowledge

Whereas in your specialist area you will have large amounts of knowledge, in this situation you will be gathering information, and therefore – as mentioned above, you need to be realistic in respect of just how much information you gather. It is important to understand that knowledge implies not only that you have information, but that you understand it and know how to apply it.

Authority

As already mentioned, to come across as an authority on a topic, you need to present yourself confidently and also present your information in a way that meets the needs and expectations of your audience. This is closely tied to your self-knowledge, since many people do not feel confident about speaking on a topic they aren't a specialist in, not matter at what level.

Empathy

This element continues to be an extremely important consideration in this situation. In order to pull together a speech that is not only going to share the information you want to share, but also meet the expectations of the audience, it is essential that you take the time to try to understand exactly what it is that the audience is expecting from you.

If we summarise the most important points from above, we can see that in considering what to share when speaking on a topic that is not a specialism of yours, there are four important things we need to take into account:

1. We need to consider how to research the topic concerned.

2. We need to consider just how much information to gather in our research, including how to recognise when to stop!

3. We need to consider what the audience is expecting to hear.

4. We need to consider how we can best present that relevant information to meet those audience needs and expectations – and potentially surpass them.

How to research a new topic

The best way for you to research a new topic really does depend on the nature of the speech you are giving. For example, if you are giving an internal speech to your organisation on its success in the last year, your research would largely consist of gathering information on what the company has achieved over the year, its finances, news reports that can be shared, other PR information, and so forth. On the other hand, if you are a psychologist who has been invited to speak at an animal welfare conference on whether the principles of psychology apply to animals in the same way as people, it is likely that you would have to do some internet research to see if there has been any other research undertaken on the topic, you may need to speak to colleagues, and so forth.

Rather than trying to give you advice for every type of scenario you may face, however, let me give you some overall advice on the best way to gather information when you are searching for information outside your company.

Before starting your research

The first step is to ensure that you understand the exact nature of what you are being asked to speak about. In the example above, are you asking to give your opinion on whether this is something you agree with, or are you being asked to validate some belief the audience already holds? Are you being asked to find new information, or comment on information being presented at the conference? Are you presenting to an audience of animal lovers or scientists? All of these questions will influence what information you research.

I recommend that you determine, as part of this, at least three questions that the audience would be seeking to have answered or addressed as part of your speech, and write these down. So, again using the above example, your three questions could be:

1. Is there such a thing as animal psychology?

2. Does this apply to all animals or just some?

3. Are the principles of animal psychology the same as for human psychology?

The number of questions you list will depend on the length and nature of your speech, but as a guideline, you should look to have one question for every ten minutes of your speech.

Undertaking an internet search

As mentioned at the beginning of this section, a particular challenge we face is that we will end up gathering too much detailed information on a topic, and end up 'drowning' ourselves in knowledge. One way to avoid doing this is to make sure that when we undertake an internet search that we search only for very specific information. This is where the questions you have drawn up as part of the previous point come into effect. When you undertake your search, make sure you enter a detailed question into your search engine. Internet search tools are very sophisticated now, and you are likely to find a far more relevant set of information if your search questions are detailed and non-ambiguous.

Undertaking a review of literature

I generally discourage people from undertaking a physical review of literature if they are seeking information for a speech. I do this for a couple of reasons. First of all, literature research takes a long time and in general the amount of time you have before a speech is insufficient for you to do an appropriate literature review as well as prepare yourself and your materials. Second, if we start reading several books, our tendency to 'information gather' may take precedence over our focus within the topic. Last, but certainly not least, is the fact that an internet search nowadays will frequently pull up a lot of salient information that would have fallen within your literature review anyway, and therefore this could well be an unnecessary waste of your time.

Knowing when to stop your research

Knowing when you have enough information is always challenging, but I have found that the best way to ensure that I do not 'over-research' is to make use of a control form as part of my research. I have included two examples of these in Toolkit Exercise 7: Knowing When to Stop Researching Your Topic (p.171) in Part 5 of the book.

Determining what the audience is expecting to hear

This process would not differ from what I detailed earlier in the chapter, other than the fact that in a way it may be easier for you to consider what you would want to know about the subject, since – actually – this could be a new subject for you too.

The final step in pulling together your speech is to determine how best to present your information to your audience. This is the topic of the next chapter.

Chapter 10

Preparation of Your Material

Now that you are comfortable with what you are going to be speaking about and the sort of focus this work should take, it is time to start pulling your material together. As I have mentioned, the purpose of this book is not so much to go through the details of how to pull together a speech, but rather to focus on some of the areas that would be rather more challenging for those of us on the autistic spectrum. That said, it is worthwhile highlighting some important considerations when pulling together your speech.

The first consideration is whether or not you want to make use of notes while speaking. Generally one tends to think about the use of notes in a presentation or speech as being quite a useful activity. I would say that this is true overall. However, from the perspective of those of us on the autistic spectrum, some additional considerations are important for us to take into account before taking the decision to actually do so.

But what we should do first of all is talk about what we actually mean by 'notes', how they are developed and how they are used in the context of public speaking.

So what do we mean by public speaking notes?

Okay, this may sound very obvious, but it may not be so to everyone – especially those people who have never undertaken any kind of presentation or public speaking activity. In general, many people – both neurotypical and autistic – find it helpful to work with lists of varying types and complexity when undertaking certain tasks. This can range from the simple 'to-do' lists that most of us keep next to us during the day in the office, through to complex checklists used by aviation pilots as they prepare their aircraft for take-off and landing. Checklists and lists are frequently invaluable in helping us ensure that we undertake all the things we had planned to – or need to – do surrounding an activity. They are brief, succinct and unambiguous. That's where their value lies.

Notes, on the other hand, tend to be slightly more extensive and detailed compared to our checklists and other 'to-do' type lists. This is where we tend to be more fluid in our thinking – we make a record of things as they pop into our heads and not necessarily in a logical order. Whereas a checklist will follow a predetermined order that it is important to follow sequentially, notes tend to be scribbled down as we are thinking of something or as we come up with ideas. Let's look at a couple of examples of what I am talking about.

Here's the 'checklist' I use when I get home from work to make sure that I feed the cats and give the relevant ones their medicine (two of them may be described as geriatric kitties, and hence the medicine!).

1. Arrive home.

2. Call cats.

3. Ensure that all are inside.

4. Take food sachets out of cupboard.

5. Dish up food for Kitty 1.

6. Add powder to Kitty 1's bowl.

7. Catch Kitty 2.

8. Administer thyroid tablet.

9. Dish up remaining foods.

10. Put down plates for Kitties in the kitchen.

11. Put down plate for Kitty in the bedroom.

12. Think about whether there is food in the house for me!

I hope the above checklist gave you a smile of recognition. I am sure if you have pets you know exactly what I mean! In any event, the purpose of the above is not so much to look at the detail of the checklist but rather to recognise the format.

On the other hand, an example of notes we take in researching our topic would be more likely to look like the following, which is a sample of the kind of ideas an author may have about a new book:

• Needs to be about 70,000 words.

• Make sure I include the character who has an autistic brother and also make sure that this brother is not only AS.

- Do some research into which agencies there are in Canada who deal with adoption of children with learning disabilities.

- Make the introduction very intriguing.

- The end needs to make people want to do something about the situation and get involved.

- The main part of the story needs to include something that makes the reader very attached to the brother, but I don't know what yet. Perhaps an accident? His own disability? Not sure.

- I need to avoid references to any particular real agency.

As you can see from the above example, the person is noting down their ideas as and when they arise. They aren't in any particular order and they are not characteristically unambiguous or simple. Also, they very obviously reflect thoughts, not fixed steps or final principles.

Okay, so let's get back to the scenario of public speaking. Is this the same sort of thing as when we talk about our public speaking notes? Well, most people, when asked to speak about something, will go away and make some notes about what they should cover. To be fair, there are many of us on the autistic spectrum who do not actually do that. We tend to 'speak from our heads'. However, our ability to do this can be both a good thing and a bad thing, as we will see a bit later when I return to the topic. But there are those of us who will make notes – and sometimes quite detailed notes as well – very much along the lines of what I have described above. However, I would propose that this is not the optimal form of public speaking notes. Public speaking notes are meant to help us focus our thinking and ensure that we speak about all we want to cover in the time we have available to us. If they have been drawn up at random, they neither focus our thinking nor ensure that we consider our timekeeping.

Like the random notes that we tend to draw up when conceptualising something (as per the example above), when we first start to think about our speech, our notes are likely to look similarly unfocused. In order for these to be useful, we need to then take the time to transfer them into a more useful format. Let's look at this first before we discuss the merits of whether or not to actually make use of notes during a speech.

Developing optimal notes for use with a speech

What are the most important steps in ensuring we create optimal notes for a speech?

When we develop notes to use with a speech, there are some important things that need to be included in those notes other than just what you want to talk about. One of these is timing. When we are undertaking public speaking, we need to keep cognisant of any time restraints or expectations in respect of our speech. Often it is not just making sure we don't over-run our speaking commitment, but also ensuring we actually speak for long enough!

Drawing up your speech outline

A question you may ask at this time is this: If I have decided not to use notes, why do I need to draw up anything? The answer is that irrespective of how good a speaker you are and how well you know your material, it is always worthwhile having a formal speech outline for the purposes of rehearsal as well as to ensure that should you have some sort of interruption in your speech, you are able to visualise the structure of your speech as a whole to be able to pick up where you left as smoothly as possible.

So what do I mean by a speech outline? This is short summary of the key sections of your speech and the high level summary of what is being covered in each of these sections. Let me go back one step before we continue. In any speech, we tend to split into a number of focus points which are called sections. In the most simple short speech, these could be:

- introduction

- main body

- conclusion.

However, most speeches will consist on average of four sections, and these will not necessarily include the introduction and conclusion. So, as an example, one of my speeches covering autism in the workplace has the following sections:

- History of employment opportunities for people on the spectrum.

- The Autism Act 2009.

- Key strengths of people on the spectrum within the workplace.

- The way forward.

You will see from this that there are four sections which flow logically into one another. In drawing up a speech outline, you need to start by identifying what your speech sections are. *If* you have never thought about this previously, the best way to consider what your sections are is to think about at which points you insert pauses. As we have already mentioned earlier, in general pauses are introduced either to make a point or to introduce a new section. I suggest that you start by noting all the areas of pause in your standard speech, and then determine whether or not these represent new sections of discussion or whether they are just pauses for emphasis.

Another thing to keep in mind when splitting your speech into sections is to consider the maximum number of elements there should be. As I mentioned previously, the ideal number of sections is four. However, depending on your topic and the duration of your speech, you could have up to six. I believe if you end up with over six sections, it is highly unlikely that these are all sections, and more likely they are a combination of sections and sub-sections.

Once you have divided your speech up into its relevant sections, the next step is to think about the key points you are going to make under each of them. These should be recorded as bullets under the section heading. Once again, depending on the nature and duration of your speech, this can vary quite a bit. However, keep in mind that you should be noting the key bullet points only, and not too much. Think of these as your 'crib notes' (for those of you familiar with the concept). They are what you need to remind you of what you need to cover under each section, without the detail behind it.

So if we go back to my breakdown of sections for my speech on Autism in the Workplace, you would find that it looks like this:

- History of employment opportunities for people on the spectrum:
    - difficulties historically
    - initial stereotypes affecting employment
    - changes over the last ten years.

- The Autism Act 2009:
    - purpose of the Act
    - implications of the Act for individuals and businesses
    - how many companies are adhering
    - outcomes of Autism Act Survey.

- Key strengths of people on the spectrum within the workplace:
    - outline of key strengths of people with ASD
    - jobs were we can add great value.

- The way forward:
  - removing the stigma going forward
  - increasing opportunities
  - what organisations can do to make a difference.

As you can see, the bullets under the sections are concise points that remind me of what else I need to say.

The final step here is to add any special comment that is important for you. For example, under a specific section you may want to make a note like 'pause for emphasis here' or 'really engage with audience here' and so forth.

Toolkit Exercise 8: Template for Developing Your Speech Notes (p.174) in Part 5 of the book provides a template for you to use in pulling together your notes. This builds on the information gathered in Toolkit Exercise 7 which was used to research your topic.

How should I record my notes?

Another important consideration is how we record these notes – is it best to record them on an A4 sheet of paper? A large index card? A few small index cards?

The best way to record your notes depends on two things. Your first consideration is what you feel comfortable with. Some people (especially those of us on the autistic spectrum) do not feel comfortable holding papers or certain types of card. If you have a sensitivity to index card paper, for example, this is obviously not an option. However, there is nothing to stop you from cutting normal paper in the same size and an index card. So take that into account first. The second consideration relates to just how many notes you have ended up with. If you have followed my guidance above, you shouldn't have too many notes. However, the need to add additional comments may have lengthened them for you. For example, if you have a large amount of notes, it may not be optimal to have your notes on an A4 sheet of paper because that paper may end up becoming too 'busy' with just too much information on it, thereby making it easier for you to lose your place. This will result in uncomfortable hesitations while you scan your notes looking for where you are meant to be. This is not a good experience for the audience.

If you are going to use notes, I recommend the use of index cards for a couple of key reasons. First, they are easier to hold in your hand while still being able to make use of your arms for any gestures you want to make, or to move around without what is in your hand distracting your audience. Small index cards will not really catch the audience's eye in any way. Second, they serve a very useful purpose in helping you to remember your pauses in between sections. If you remember the discussion earlier in the book around the importance of pauses at key points in your speech, you should recognise what I mean by this. If you put the details of each section on a separate card, you will know what you are covering in that section by glancing at that single card (and the back of that card if there are a number of notes) and the fact that you are only seeing what is relevant for that particular section automatically puts you in the mindset of ending 'at the end of the card'. If you are nervous about speaking and possibly tend to speak a little too fast, the brief period of time that it will take you to turn to your next index card and scan it will force you to pause where you intended to pause in the first place, thereby reducing the risk of 'express train speeches'.

To note or not to note? That is the question

Consider whether or not you find it useful to make use of notes, a question I have alluded to in a number of areas in the book. Ultimately, this is a question you need to answer for yourself, but to help you make that decision, I have broken down the question into some of the positives and negatives of the practice of using notes, starting with the latter. I will end by sharing my own observations, with the repeated proviso that this needs to be your own decision about how best you feel you can speak publicly.

The negatives of using notes
HIDING BEHIND YOUR NOTES

One of the biggest negatives of using notes is the potential for a nervous speaker to bury themselves in their notes rather than address the audience. By this I mean that they avoid eye contact and often hold their notes in such a way that the audience cannot really see their faces, or at the very most, infrequently.

READING NOT SPEAKING

A person can end up reading from their notes rather than speaking to their audience, resulting in them skipping to a 'monotone reading' mode rather than an interactive speech mode. The likely result is that your audience will become bored with your speech and disengage.

LACK OF PROJECTION

Linked to the above, a person can end up talking as if to themselves rather than projecting their voice forward to the audience. This can result in the audience straining to hear what is being said, potentially not hearing most of your speech and ultimately switching off altogether.

LACK OF ENGAGEMENT

This is the greatest risk with using notes if they are used incorrectly, namely that you will not engage effectively with your audience. You will see that Chapter 13 in Part 4 of the book is dedicated to engaging your audience, and when you get to this chapter, you will have reinforced just how important engagement is. Suffice to say at this point that if you are overly dependent on reading your notes, engagement will just not happen.

Positives of using notes
GOOD VISUAL REMINDER OF YOUR SPEECH FLOW

A very good reason for using notes is that they provide us with a visual reminder of the flow and direction of our speech. Sometimes, despite practising our speech to what we consider to be perfection, when we arrive at the venue and start speaking, we end up mixing up the order of our speech without realising that this could have a significant effect on our overall timing or impact. Notes will help you remember the intended flow of information.

GOOD TO HELP YOU ENTER YOUR SECTION PAUSES

Notes can be extremely useful if you find that you are running away with yourself during your speech in terms of speed. As we practise, we can get so familiar with the material that we almost take it for granted that some of the basic information will already have been picked up by audiences, or that they are as familiar with this as we are. As a result, we tend to eliminate some of the important pauses that we originally built into our speeches. By using notes, we ensure that we retain the section breaks. Even if you don't consider that this will be a problem for you, it is always a useful service.

GOOD VISUAL REMINDER OF POINTS OF EMPHASIS

Notes are very useful if you have certain points in your speech at which you want to add additional emphasis, action or visuals. On an index card, you can make a note next to the point where this needs to be done, whereas speaking without notes, you run the risk of forgetting. This means you will either completely miss the opportunity or will try to insert it somewhere else, which could end up sounding disjointed or completely inappropriate.

GOOD TOOL TO KEEP A TREMBLY HAND STILL

If you find that you suffer from the nervous trembles, holding an index card in your hand can help to disguise that tremble so that it does not distract your audience.

GOOD TOOL FOR FIDGETY HANDS

Similarly, if you find that you have a tendency to fidget with your hand (tapping your leg, fiddling with your hair or clothes, etc.), holding an index card discreetly will keep your hand occupied. Even playing with your cards a little will be less distracting than playing your body, clothes, hair or jewellery.

GOOD TOOL FOR STRESS MANAGEMENT

The one thing I do like about using index cards is that they can be used as a hidden stress management tool! If you find that you are beginning to have some sort of an overload, you probably are aware that a significant part of coping with it and keeping it under control relates to your ability to put your focus on something else that is less stressful. I have found that I can use the index cards as a type of 'pressure ball' to help me focus on something physical that has a neutral effect on me. So, for example, I can gently squeeze the cards with my fingertips, and then release them. Squeeze and release. Move them to your other hand. Then squeeze and release. Squeeze and release again. With practice beforehand, this is something that you will be able to do while still continuing with your speech – and no-one in the audience will even know that you are doing it. Work out what works best for you.

I hope that the above has made you think about using notes based on criteria a little broader than purely the value they represent to remind you of your speech. You may want to try a couple of information speaking events where you determine whether or not using notes works for you.

The use of visuals and slides

If you are going to use slides or other visuals for your speech, there are a couple of very important considerations in drawing them up. Let us speak about some of the practicalities of pulling together a slide pack for your speech.

Do a good job, or do nothing at all

Most important of all is that unless you can do something of very high quality, do nothing at all. As I have already mentioned in Chapter 7, a visual slide or presentation will have far more impact on the audience than your actual speech, so if it is of low quality or badly constructed, it will end up disillusioning your audience. They will see your presentation as an extension of you and your personal skills. If your presentation is sloppy or outdated, they will start to see you as sloppy and out of touch. If your presentation is too busy (i.e. it contains too much information on each slide), people will start to think that you are a bad communicator. Do you see why it is so important?

Limit the number of slides

Don't make the mistake of drawing up a slide deck of 20 slides! Audiences are just not interested in that much information. Twenty plus slides reaches the area of information overload. I generally recommend that for an hour-long speech, the MAXIMUM number of slides should be eight to ten, although – depending on the nature of the slides – you may be able to get away with 12. What I mean by this is that sometimes you will have slides that are brief 'attention-grabbers' with no real content, used purely to focus your audience's attention or introduce some humour. For example, an attention-grabber slide for a section of your speech called 'climbing the slippery slope of career progression' could be a photograph of a bear sliding down a snow covered hill. This will make audiences relax and laugh. It isn't something you are going to leave on the screen for long, and therefore it takes up only a short period of your 'screen' time.

Don't put too many words on a slide

People are there to listen to you speak, not to read a presentation off the screen. Your slides are intended to be visual enhancement for your speaking, not repetition of what you are saying. If you are speaking on a topic about which you are aware people will want to have details, prepare some handouts and advise the audience at the start of your speech that handouts will be available at the end of your speech containing all the information covered in the speech. This will reassure them that they do not have to make their own notes – another distraction you want to avoid.

Do not make your slides too busy

Your slides should never contain so much information or detail that your audience can end up getting swallowed up by it. For example, if you want to show a slide representing university learning, put up a photo of a lecture hall with a lot of detail and you will find that the audience (some more than others) will end up disconnecting from what you are saying to examine the details of the picture, notice people in the seats, have a look at what they can see on the board, and so forth. On the other hand, if you put up the image of a graduation hat, people know what you are focusing on, but are not distracted.

Cover one idea per slide or per visible part of the slide

The last thing you want to do is to have too many ideas up on the screen at one time. Apart from the fact that this can be overwhelming for the audience, it also encourages the audience to move ahead of you in their thinking while you are still speaking about the first idea!

However, we have already cautioned against having too many slides. You do not need a situation where you have 30 slides, each with their own idea! In any event, if that did happen, that would indicate to me that you were trying to cover too much in your visuals. Remember – not every idea needs a visual!

Sometimes you may have a number of ideas that you want to present on a single slide. Let me give you a practical example. Say you are doing a presentation on the composition of the employee reward package. Your key idea in one section is to clarify the components of the employee's package. Now, for those of you who are not familiar with employee pay and reward, don't worry – I am just using this as an example! But to fully explain my example, I need to give a little detail.

Say I want to explain that an employee's reward package is made up of the following elements:

- base pay (salary)

- benefits (e.g. pension)

- voluntary benefits (e.g. buying things at a discount from the company)

- incentives and bonuses.

As I go through each one of these bullets, I want to spend some time explaining what the item is. Now, if we went for the principle that each new idea needs to be on a new slide, this would mean we needed to have four slides – and that takes up a lot of your 'slide-time'. A better way would be to enter all of the details into one slide, but have the different element 'pop up' only when you click on your pointer or mouse.

So in the previous example, you would end up with a single slide up on the screen which would initially appear like this:

Figure 10.1 First element

You would explain that there are various elements of total reward, and then use your cursor to change the slide to look like this:

Figure 10.2 Second element

Once again, you would explain your addition to the slide and then move to the next one, as the following few slides indicate:

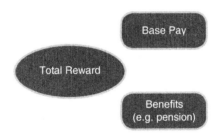

Figure 10.3 Third element

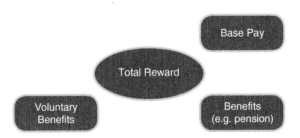

Figure 10.4 Fourth element

Figure 10.5 Full slide

Now you have the full slide. Can you see how this would save you time in terms of the number of slides to present?

Try to avoid slides that are too distracting

Now don't misunderstand what I am saying here! Your slides need to be of high quality and impactful. However, they must not distract from what you are actually saying. The audience is there first and foremost to hear you speak. If you have a slide that is particularly eye catching or impactful, pause your speech and allow your audience to take it in before continuing. If it is likely to be a slightly longer pause so that people can either watch some sort of visual or read something, I suggest you actually say, 'I'll pause for a couple of moments to let you take that in…' or something to that effect.

Practise, practise, practise

With the use of visuals, it is incredibly important that you practise the timing of your speech using the slides, as well as timings to move to new slides. This needs to be almost automatic for you, because you do not want to be focusing your attention on the screen behind you when you are up on the stage. Doing so gives the audience the impression that you are using the overheads to remind yourself what to say. You should feel confident enough to be able to click to go to the next without even looking at the screen, or by viewing it discreetly out of the corner of your eye.

Have a backup

If you are taking some sort of electronic slides, have a backup with you. If you are carrying them on a USB memory stick, have a second stick with a duplicate version. If you have forwarded the slide pack to the venue ahead of time, still bring a version on your own USB stick. You will never regret having a backup, but you certainly will regret *not* having one!

Linking notes and visuals

Using iPads and other electronic notebooks as a source of your notes can also have the added advantage of being able to link to the visual presentation your audience sees. Whether or not this is a good thing depends very much on the type of audience, what you are speaking about and just how 'visual' your presentation is.

Now that we have spoken about how to optimally prepare your material, we should take some time to think about your own personal preparation ahead of the event. This is the topic of the next chapter.

Chapter 11

Personal Preparation

Up to this point we have focused on your preparation from the perspectives of getting your topic and materials ready, as well as preparing yourself psychologically. It is also very important for us to consider our preparation for public speaking from one additional perspective – our personal presentation.

There are three key elements of personal presentation, namely:

- clothes

- grooming

- personal presentation style.

We have already discussed the final of these bullets, namely personal presentation style, under the heading of public speaking persona. However, the elements of clothing and grooming are very important to consider. When you present yourself to your audience, you aim to show them someone who is professional and credible. I am the last one to say that people need to 'fit in' when it comes to anything. I personally consider myself to be a unique individual, and my style of dress may not always be what people expect in some situations. I also recognise that there are times when it absolutely is appropriate to dress more in line with what is expected, since not to do so would be confusing for the people around me. As an example, I generally like to wear quite colourful blouses at times. However, if I am attending a funeral, I recognise that this would not be appropriate, and I would adjust my clothing style to fit the occasion.

In a similar vein, if we are speaking professionally, we need to take into account the environment and the ambience of the event we are attending. Much as a person may feel comfortable in casual clothing, if this is a black tie event this would just make the person stand out, and could potentially make them lose their credibility as a speaker. You need to develop your own unique presentation attire that – while uniquely you – is not radically different from what people attending the event are expecting to see in a speaker.

Make sure that you are comfortable

The most important consideration for you as a public speaker – especially a public speaker with potential sensory issues – is that you need to be comfortable in what you are wearing. Although the reason for this may seem obvious, I would also remind you that if you are uncomfortable in your outfit, this will come across in your body language. As we discussed in Chapter 7, this can have a negative effect on how inspirational or charismatic you appear. You could end up being perceived as a nervous or unconfident speaker – all because of an uncomfortable outfit!

If you are sensitive to certain materials or styles of clothes, in some cases this may mean that you need to do a lot of preparation. For example, if you are uncomfortable in tight suits and yet are speaking at a very formal business event that expects you to wear a tuxedo, you may need to invest in having one made for you by a tailor, using material that you know is not going to irritate your skin, and to dimensions that you find comfortable. Make sure that you have organised this well in advance of your actual speaking engagement. Although this will be a potential expense for you, if you intend to make a career of your public speaking, you really should see this as a very positive investment, since you will use it more than once.

If you intend to wear something that you don't usually wear, consider the effect this could have on you. As an example more familiar to the ladies, are you going to be wearing high heels when you don't regularly wear them? If so, do yourself a big favour and make sure that you practise walking around in your shoes so that you do not end up spraining your ankle on stage because your ankles are not used to walking with 'heels' on.

Similarly, if you buy new shoes, make sure that you test drive them first. There is nothing worse that walking around with 'new-shoe-blisters' at a post-speech networking event – believe me, I know! Also, if you are wearing jewellery you haven't worn before, try it out first. You will be surprised how many of us have skin reactions to certain pieces of jewellery. Test your accessories out well in advance of the date of your speech.

Make sure you are professionally 'groomed'

As I have already said, even if you feel that the event you are presenting at is not so high profile, you need to think about what image you want to project as a speaker. Do you want to be seen as a casual speaker? Do you want to be seen as a high impact professional? Or do you want to be seen somewhere in between the two? How you have developed your speaking persona very much determines your thinking around your personal presentation. Whether you decide to be highly professional or more casual, your physical presentation needs to be professional.

When you present to an audience, they are going to be observing you for the entire time. People have an automatic habit of assessing others according to how they present themselves. We have already spoken about clothing, but you need to make sure that you also take care of your personal grooming. As a public speaker, you don't want to have unkempt or uncut hair, stubble on your chin or smeared make-up. This is something that can make a huge impact on your audience's perception of you. Let me highlight a couple of considerations, breaking this down into ladies versus gents.

Ladies
MAKE-UP

The bane of my life! I seriously am not someone who normally wears make-up, but I do recognise that if I am going to be speaking at an event where I am standing on a stage under a bright light and where I am potentially being video-taped – yes, I need to wear some make-up or risk looking like a ghost! You will probably find the same applies to you. If you, like me, do not wear make-up often, make sure that you have found a brand that does not irritate your skin or eyes, and that you practise wearing it for at least a week before your event so that your body acclimates to wearing it during the day. You may also want to get some instruction on how to apply make up professionally, or have your make-up done for you on the day. If you do have it done for you, make sure you have had the opportunity beforehand to try out the person doing the application so that you are happy with their style. Also make sure they use your make-up and brushes rather than theirs.

NAILS

Doing your nails is a must – whether you have them painted, manicured or false nails applied! I am not saying that you have to wear nail polish: what I am saying is that you need to make sure that at the minimum your nails have been cleaned and tidied. If you speak at predominantly business or professional events, you may want to consider nail polish or nail extensions.

HAIR

If you have long hair, you may want to get your hair professionally styled before the event. Always make sure that your hair is neat and tidy, because people looking at your face can be distracted by fly-away hair.

Gentlemen
SHAVING

If you are clean-shaven rather than having a beard, it is really important that you ensure that you are clean-shaven on the day of your speech. Even if you are trying to grow a beard, starting just before you are going to have a speaking event isn't a good idea, so you may have to sacrifice any stubble-growth until after your event.

If you have a beard and/or moustache, on the other hand, make sure that you have them trimmed and tidied. Being on your face, these can be highly distracting to the audience, so make sure they are under control.

NAILS

Yes, even gentlemen need to do their nails! As a person going up to stand in front of an audience, you need to make sure your nails have been cleaned and tidied. Don't let chipped, dirty or overly long nails distract your audience.

HAIR

Make sure that your hair has been washed and trimmed appropriately. Even if you have short hair, it can grow out of its style very quickly and end up looking tatty. You may want to consider going to your barber or stylist on the morning of your event, or the day before.

Most of all, make sure that you are happy with the way you look and that your presentation fits with the speaking persona you have developed. Your image reflects *you* and you need to ensure that – while being professional – you are not trying to be false. Recognise and identify how you look and feel as being your *public speaking me*.

Chapter 12

Practical Issues before You Speak Publicly

Up to this point we have focused largely on your personal preparation and the preparation of your material ahead of a public speaking engagement. In this chapter I focus on an element of public speaking preparation that I have found over the years to be particularly useful as an individual on the autistic spectrum: the more practical issues surrounding your speaking engagement's venue, physical environment and presentation expectations. Although some of these may be considered trivial or superfluous for most neurotypicals, they really do need to be considered by those of us on the spectrum to ensure we do not become stressed unnecessarily. Small though they may be, they can make the difference between an individual stepping forward to speak confidently and a person suffering an overwhelming case of sensory overload due to an unexpected situation.

When we commit to a public speaking engagement, the mechanism for this can vary considerably depending on the circumstances under which it has been pulled together, as any seasoned speaker will know. The engagement may be a formal public speaking event, an impromptu media presentation or a presentation to staff called at reasonably short notice due to a key corporate event. In some cases you will have had months of preparation time, in others a couple of hours – if that! This chapter is largely focused on those events where you have time ahead of the engagement to prepare and follow the recommended steps below. However, the same principles can apply to any speaking arrangement, and I will recommend later in the chapter what you can do if you are called to speak publicly at short notice.

So what are some of the essential things that you should try to make sure you have found out and prepared for ahead of your speaking engagement? First let me give you a hypothetical example of the sorts of things I am speaking about.

Case study: Potential challenges of sensory overload

Vicki and Paul were two members of their regional autism support group and had been involved with trying to raise the profile of the charity in order to help raise funds for the organisation. Both Vicki and Paul had high-functioning autism, although Vicki felt very strongly about referring to her condition as Asperger syndrome rather than as an ASD. Paul, on the other hand, had no time for labels and really did not care what people called him, so long as they acknowledged his unique contributions in the organisation and in society as a whole.

As part of their efforts to raise the profile of the organisation, both Vicki and Paul had been involved in a number of small fund raising events, such as a sponsored 'Bring your pet to work' day, a sponsored lactose and gluten-free cake sale (which proved extremely popular) and a sponsored computer game marathon. All of these had been highly successful in raising funds of the charity, and a lot of people had signed up to become regular donors.

One day, the head of the regional support unit, Robert, called Vicki and Paul into his office.

'You two should be very proud of yourselves, you know,' Robert started, smiling at the two people in front of him.

'We are,' said Vicki, not sure why Robert had made such an obvious observation.

Robert paused a moment, and then gave a small laugh.

'Yes. Yes, of course you are, Vicki. All right, let me get to the point. I have been contacted by the local paper. They are running a conference next month talking about community development and support within the local community for people with needs. They have asked me to invite you to speak at the event on some of the work you have been doing.'

Paul frowned. 'Why?'

'Because they felt that the public would like to hear from you, and they recognise that what you have been doing in raising funds is something really important and valuable.'

'Of course it is,' interrupted Vicki. 'Or we wouldn't have been doing it. I don't know what other people want to hear about, though.'

Robert smiled again. 'Actually, I think they would really like to hear about you – about how you came to be where you are today, what it is like being autistic, why the work of the charity is important for you.'

Vicki frowned and started objecting, 'I don't see why. That's my business and I don't understand…'

'I understand,' Paul interrupted. 'It's so that neurotypical people can get to see us directly and understand a bit more about the people they could be supporting, yeah?'

Robert nodded emphatically. 'Yes Paul! Exactly! And it would be really good for us if you were to do this, since it would highlight some of the work that we do, and show the public that we have some really talented and intelligent people in our own autistic community as well.'

Paul nodded. 'I will do it.'

Robert looked at Vicki expectantly. She sighed. 'Yeah, okay. But I don't know what I'm supposed to be talking about…'

A month later, Vicki and Paul were on their way to the conference venue. Robert had spent quite a lot of time with Vicki helping her to pull together her speech, and she was now confident in what she was going to speak about and how she was going to present herself. Paul, on the other hand, had confidently drawn up an outline of what he wanted to speak about and was happy to leave it at that. He had practised his speech a couple of times in front of Robert in their local church (only because it had a pulpit, which was useful as representing a conference podium) and Robert had been very impressed with his natural public speaking skills.

Eventually they arrived at the conference centre and made their way to where they had been advised the speakers were to meet. They walked there slowly, Paul looking around nervously. This really wasn't what he had expected. The venue was largely an open-ground event with one large tent in the centre of a field. It reminded Paul somewhat of a circus, and that thought made him uncomfortable and ill at ease. Vicki walked steadfastly beside Paul. Fortunately for her, she was not as strongly affected by the open spaces as Paul was, and the thought of speaking in a large tent held no reservations for her in the way that it did for Paul.

Reaching the side entrance, they entered the tent and sat down beside two other people, presumably also speakers at the event. The organiser came and introduced herself as being Katie, and explained that she would come and call them to stage individually when it was time for them to come and speak. Both Vicki and Paul indicated that this was all right and that they understood, but Paul could feel himself starting to get stressed. The venue was very noisy, and the walls of the tent kept swaying in the breeze, causing a visual distraction for him that he had not expected ahead of the event.

Vicki noticed Paul starting to stim and turned to him. 'Try to focus, Paul. It will be over soon.'

Paul stared at her unhearing. Vicki tutted and turned to look at her notes. After a few minutes the conference started – and both Paul and Vicki jumped. The organisers were using an old loud-speaker system that emitted high-frequency, piercing squeals that – while probably not that noticeable to the average neurotypical – were highly noticeable to Vicki and Paul's highly sensitive ears. Paul dropped down onto his knees and covered his ears, the sharp sounds creating an agonising pain in his head. Paul had highly sensitive hearing, and this sound system made it impossible for him to do anything other than clutch his head and fold down into a ball. The conference chair had been speaking for a while, and was obviously preparing to call their first guest.

Katie popped her head around the curtain. 'Paul? You're up next. Paul?'

Paul wasn't even able to lift his head to acknowledge Katie's prompt. Slowly he staggered to his feet and made his way out of the tent and into the open air. Katie stared after him in horror.

'Where's he going?' she asked Vicki, who was sitting on a chair nearby.

'He's had an overload. He won't be coming back.'

Katie stared at Vicki for a minute, then quickly turned back into the main part of the tent, obviously distressed. Vicki thought she heard Katie speaking briefly to someone else, and then another announcement was made, inviting Vicki to join them at the front. Katie's head popped around the curtain, a weak smile on her face.

'You now!' she said, with a voice that struck Vicki as being slightly different to the one she had originally used to introduce herself. Vicki moved past her into the tent and made her way to the stage. Then she stopped. She blinked her eyes and let her eyes dart around the front of the tent. Where was the podium? Vicki felt her heart begin to race as she struggled to process this unexpected information. The venue was an open-plan tent with a small stage. However, there was no podium, and speakers were being handed a hand-held microphone as they went up onto the stage.

Vicki felt herself panicking. What was she going to do with her notes? How was she going to read her notes and turn the pages while holding a microphone? Worst of all, how was she going to use her usual coping mechanism (moving from foot to foot very rapidly) without a podium? With a podium there her coping strategy was hardly noticeable.

With nothing there she would be totally exposed to an audience of a couple of hundred people.

Vicki reached the stage and accepted the microphone with a trembling hand. She stared at it silently, struggling to get herself into a place where she could focus on speaking. She noticed that the audience, previously silent, was starting to make subtle mumbling noises, and she swallowed hard. But try as she might, she was unable to start speaking, as exposed as she was in the middle of the stage. After five minutes she turned and stepped down from the stage and made her way to the exit.

'What have I done?' she asked herself. 'I've just let everyone down. What's the matter with me?'

It is very easy for people on the spectrum reading the above case study to identify with the sensory overload effects that were experienced by Paul and Vicki. While this scenario described an example of what could happen, the possibility of unexpected overloads can be greatly reduced if you take the time to prepare for your speaking arrangement beforehand by doing some initial preparatory work. You can do this by asking the following questions, either to the organiser or to yourself as you do your research.

Where is the venue?

This may seem like a very obvious question, but it is not as obvious as it appears at first glance. You need to know where the venue is: you need to understand the *physical environment* your engagement is situated *within*.

As you saw from this case study, environmental factors can play havoc with your senses if you are not expecting or prepared for them. When you agree to speak at a conference, you need to understand what sort of environment you will be expected to speak in. Will it be in a small seminar room? A large conference room? An arena? Or is it going to be some sort of open-air event, such as an outdoor conference or the type described in this case study? Each of these different venues will present you with different sensory stimuli, and unless you are prepared for them, you could really struggle.

Part of understanding how this type of venue will be relevant to you is to make sure you understand what your hypersensitivities are and how you react when these are overstimulated. You will have considered part of this in previous toolkit exercises from earlier in the book, but it may be worthwhile outlining here some of the causes of sensory overload associated with the different types of environment. Keep in mind, however, this is in no way intended to be a definitive list, and will very much depend on your own personal sensitivities.

Small seminar room or office

A small seminar room or office can be the least challenging to people on the spectrum. However, sometimes it can present a challenge if there are a lot of people in a small space, since this would mean that this could end up being quite noisy, and it is likely that the audience will be situated a lot closer to you than if they were in a larger space. In addition, it is likely that this sort of space will not have a stage, making you on the same level as the audience. Some people with ASD can see this as quite challenging, since the audience is close and rather more intimate than we would prefer. However, if you prepare yourself for this and develop some strategies to deal with it, you will cope far better than if you leave it to chance.

Another point to keep in mind with this sort of environment is that there tends to be no breakaway area for you as a speaker. So once you have finished speaking, you will generally be expected to take a seat in the audience while the other speakers finish or until the event is over. As many of us prefer to try to 'get some space' after the actual speech, this is again something you need to be aware of so that you are able to cope with it.

A lecture hall

You may consider that this is the same as a conference room or seminar room, but there is one difference with most lecture halls that it is worth noting. Let me explain this by referring to an experience of my own. At the time I had been speaking publicly for a while and was quite comfortable with the process and most types of venue. One day, however, I was asked to do a formal presentation for a client company, addressing some of its senior staff in the Cambridge office. I had assumed that I would be addressing them in one of the company meeting rooms, all of which I was familiar with. However, on arriving I was informed that the venue had been changed and that we were going to be using the nearby university instead. I was a little uncomfortable at not having had the opportunity to look at the venue beforehand, but – having spoken in almost every type of venue by that time – I didn't think it would be too much of an issue. Well, I was wrong! When we went into the reserved lecture theatre, I was confronted with a venue which had a series of chairs arranged in a semi-circular fashion, going downhill towards the podium which was situated at the bottom and centre of the semi-circle. For those of you who have attended university, you will be familiar with the typical lecture hall, but for anyone who has not been in a lecture hall, another way to picture this is to think of a cinema theatre. You have the entrance at the top of an incline, with the chairs leading downwards (although this tends not to be in a semi-circle) with the front right down at the bottom.

For me, I found I was not prepared for this type of venue for two main reasons. First of all, I was faced with a bunch of people staring down at me rather than me looking down at them. This can make a surprising difference to the way speak and how you feel during your speech. I found that it left me initially feeling more vulnerable than when I was above, or even at the same level as, my audience. Second, many of us on the autistic spectrum do have a challenge with eye contact in any event. When we speak to people either at the same level or below us, this is easier to manage, since your range of vision tends to be level and downwards, rather than upwards. However, when you have your audience sitting above you, it is far more of a challenge to maintain that eye (or face) contact, since it is very easy to start dropping your eyes down to 'level and below'. This can give the audience the impression that you lack confidence. You can end up focusing on a very narrow range of people at the lowest levels in the theatre which – again – can give the impression of lack of confidence and also make those people you are staring at feel very uncomfortable.

If you know you are going to be speaking at a venue such as this, make sure that you take some time speaking in this sort of an environment. Even if you cannot find another lecture theatre to practise in, there are ways to improvise. A good example, if you live in a duplex or double storey house, is to stand in the back garden and try to make your speech addressing someone in the upstairs window. This will be an exaggeration for you, since most theatres are not quite so high, but it will help you become familiar with the different ways you need to hold yourself and project your voice when speaking upwards.

A large conference room

With a large conference room, it is more likely that there will be a stage, given the size of the venue. There will probably be some sort of audio system, with microphones and speakers. There may be formal conference lighting, and if the event is taking place at night this could be quite intense.

Above all, be prepared for the size of the audience. I have seen many people, who are completely at ease with speaking, freeze at the sight of hundreds of bodies in seats in front of them.

Also, be aware of the potential noise level from such a large venue. While this will certainly settle down once you actually start to speak, the level of noise while you are approaching the stage or preparing to speak can be surprising and can build up your stress levels unnecessarily.

Speaking in an arena

We are sometimes called to speak in a very large arena. This type of speaking can be very intimidating, because there are a number of things we need to take into account which we may not be expecting. The first of these is what I call the echo-effect. If you have ever been a member of the audience in an arena, you will be very aware of the echo that tends to resonate as the public speaker booms away. If you watch the person speaking (if you are fortunate enough to be near enough to see them!) you will see that their mouths are not in sync with what is coming through the loud speaker system. In other words, there is a time-lag between what the person says and when the audience gets to hear it. As a member of the audience, this is not too big a deal and we handle it – in general – with no particular issues. However, as a speaker, it is important to keep in mind that your audience is sometimes a few seconds behind you. You could be discussing something and want to give a visual example (or joke) linked to what you are saying. However, if you do not pause to allow the audio to catch up with your visuals, all that you will do is confuse and potentially irritate your audience. Speaking in an arena environment requires far more pauses than speaking in any other environment and you need to make sure you are comfortable speaking this way and can do it in a way that still flows for the people listening.

Another related issue that can cause a problem is the loud-speaker system itself. Often these do have high frequency emissions or 'squeals' that can be particularly painful for many of us. I struggle with this: it literally feels like someone putting a red hot poker through my head (not that I know what this feels like, but I can surmise…). So in my case I wear earplugs – the sort that do not cut out all sound (not that any earplugs cut out all sound for me) but which soften those high frequency noises to a level I can cope with.

It is highly likely that floodlights will be in use. Floodlights can be painful to visually sensitive people, as well as highly distracting as they move around. Once again, make sure that you prepare for this. If you are highly sensitive visually, you may want to consider wearing some lightly tinted sunglasses or glasses.

An open-air event

If you are speaking in an outdoor or very open environment, this can sometimes result in a lot of visual and auditory distractions. Unlike speaking in a more controlled environment, there will be a lot more noise – both from the audience and from the general area around you – and there will be a lot more to be distracted by visually. Also, if you have sensitivity to bright light or skin sensitivities to direct sunlight, and so on, this could be a problem if you are not prepared.

What is the format of the speaking venue?

Consider whether there is a stage, whether there is a podium or an open stage, whether you are being filmed or not, and whether there is panel seating or not.

No stage

I have spoken about most of the reasons to be aware of a situation where there is no stage in the sections above covering the venues such as a small seminar room/office or a lecture theatre and in the case study. Consider:

- *How close will your audience be?* If they are in a small seminar room or office, it is likely that you do not need to project your voice as strongly as you would if you were in a lecture hall or a larger conference hall with a public speaking system.

- *Where do you go when you have finished speaking?* As mentioned, in smaller environments you will generally find that you are expected to just join the audience by sitting in the front row (usually reserved for speakers). Make sure you are prepared to remain in the room after your session – have something to drink with you, and something to focus on if this helps you to relax, such as a notebook so that you can write or doodle, for example.

Podium versus open stage

Try to find out in advance whether the venue has a podium or is an open-stage format. This is important for you for a number of reasons. First, if you have decided to use notes, it is useful to know whether you can use larger papers or whether you need to make these small 'crib notes' that you hold in your hand. If it is the latter, you also need to make sure that you have practised speaking holding these in your hand so that you look natural, and are not seen to be overly dependent on your notes, since they will be far more visible if there is no podium. Another consideration is that if you are attending somewhere that has no podium but also expects the speakers to hold a microphone, you need to make sure you are able to shuffle your cards without making a noise on the microphone or actually dropping your cards! It can be challenging, and sometimes it can be better to have just a single, slightly larger card in this situation where you list very concise bullet points as reminders of your key points. That way the majority of your time is spent addressing the audience directly rather than looking down at your notes.

Another reason why some people prefer to have a podium is because they feel 'protected' from the audience. The podium acts as a physical barrier between them and the audience and – particularly for those people on the spectrum who struggle with physical contact – this can be a significant support tool. Finding out that you do not have the physical barrier can be intimidating, leaving you feeling vulnerable and exposed. You could suddenly become far more aware of your posture and body language than you need to be, and this could have a very negative effect on your confidence and ability to speak. If you know there is the chance that there will be no podium and you are a person who prefers to have that barrier, you need to develop another strategy to maintain distance between yourself and your audience. This can be by making use of movement. If you are delivering a speech and slowly move on the stage, this can have the effect of dissipating tension and can reassure you that you are the one who is distanced from the audience while they are anchored to their chairs. Walking a few steps to the left, then back to the centre, then a few steps to the right will help you to subconsciously acknowledge that the audience is not physically following you. Their eyes may be following you (or they certainly should be if you are making an impact!), but they are remaining in their seats, and therefore the distances between them and you are regularly changing, and therefore in your control. Movement also has the positive effect of dissipating energy that may be building up due to tension. Just keep the movement smooth and not overly fast. There is nothing worse than attending an event where the speaker briskly moves one way and another as he or she speaks. You end up giving your audience an 'energetic-speaker-related whiplash'.

On the other hand, there are many of us who prefer to be able to move around when we speak. I, personally, prefer to be able to move a little as I am speaking and therefore do not particularly like using a podium, which tends to anchor you to a particular spot. If you are like me and prefer to move around a bit, find out from the organiser how much flexibility you have to move. For example, many podiums have a microphone that is powerful enough for you to be able to move a few steps to the left and right without sound quality being compromised. However, if the speech is being filmed by a static camera which has a close angle, the organisers will want you to stay quite close to the podium. In this case, you will need to make sure you have other coping mechanisms to handle any discomfort you experience due to standing on the spot. I tend to make up for my lack of leg movement by using my arms more, and if I have been asked not to be too 'flappy' with my arms due to filming, I tend to hold onto the sides of the podium (like the proverbial preacher!), although this is not my preferred style. In any event, you need to know what you are going to do ahead of the event. Practise at home doing a full session standing still in one spot and – if you are able – ask someone you trust to give you feedback on what you do with your body during this time. You may find that you start doing things with your body that you weren't aware of and which could be distracting for an audience, such as swaying your hips or rocking backwards and forward on your heels. Once you know you are doing these things, you can practise other more appropriate body language which minimises the chances of you continuing to do this.

Sessions being filmed or not

It is always good to know whether the organiser intends to videotape the event or not. There are a number of reasons for this, least of which is that you should ensure that you are entitled to a copy of your filmed speech and have the right to use it on your website or blog without any charges or restrictions. Bear in mind that it can make a big difference as to how you speak if you are being filmed. First of all, it is highly likely that they will use far more lighting than in a general speaking event. You need to ensure that you are prepared for that as far as your hypersensitivities go. They could require you to stay in a very small space throughout your speech, whereas you had planned to move around. Sometimes, if you speak to the organiser beforehand, you can agree with them the optimal zoom for the cameras which would allow you to move as you normally do, or the organiser could arrange for the camera to be on a flexible stand which allows it to follow you as you move around. But most of the time the cameras tend to be fixed and inflexible, so you need to improvise in terms of how much you move. Be aware of where the camera is so that you can make sure that you are facing in that direction for the majority of your speech.

Occasionally, you may be asked to do a public speaking event by webinar or purely by being filmed. I have always found this more challenging. I find it very difficult to picture an audience of several hundred (or even thousand) when I am effectively talking to a single camera! The format of the filming may also create a challenge for you as well. For example, several years ago I was taking part in a public speaking event where international speakers were being recorded in their home countries and their speeches played on the big screens on the day of the event. The camera crew came through to my offices to record me speaking in one of our conference rooms. The person directing the recording of the video told me to start and I turned to the camera and started speaking to my virtual audience. The cameraman immediately stopped me at this point and told me not to look directly at the camera, but to rather look across the room so that the camera could film me looking across at an invisible audience. While I understood what he was asking me to do, try as I might I found it incredibly hard not to turn to look at my actual audience at that time, which was the cameraman, and we ended up having to redo take after take after take, by which time my speech felt artificial and totally compromised. Eventually I had to take a stand and tell the cameraman that we either recorded the video the way I needed to speak, or we did without my speech. Ultimately, they ended up using my speech where I looked at the camera only a few times, but personally I was never really satisfied with it because I came across as strained and artificial – quite the opposite of my usual speaking persona.

The use of speaker panel seating or not

Panel seating is where the conference speakers are asked to sit up on the stage at a panel type desk, so that the audience can see them throughout the conference. It is very important for you to know if you are going to be required to do this at a conference.

First of all, it will require you to sit potentially quite close to someone for quite a long period of time. Many of us are not comfortable sitting close to others, and can find this sort of environment stressful.

Second, when you have finished your speech you could well be slightly overloaded and want to get into your quiet space or breakaway area. If you are required to remain on the stage, sitting next to at least one other person, under the bright lights and be stared at by the audience, this may become very stressful for you.

If you have concerns about the need to do this, do not just be quiet about it, but speak to your organiser. They could arrange, for example, for you to sit at the end of the stage panel so that you are free to slip away should you feel the need. I often find that just being able to do this removes the challenge for me, and I then am able to remain there the entire time. However, if you feel that you really cannot stay on stage after your speech, they may arrange for you to either speak first or last, and to leave the stage at that time. The important thing is to arrange this in advance with the organiser. They need to understand that you have requirements, and if you are going to participate in the event, there are certain things that need to be taken into account to accommodate you.

Lighting and audiovisual equipment

Check the type of lighting used in the venue. Are they going to use spotlights on the stage? If the event is an award ceremony or such like, are they intending to make use of colourful changes in lighting or strobe lighting (for example, when calling people to the front)? Will the venue make use of strong fluorescent lighting? I do not need to explain to you why it is important for you to know about this beforehand if you have any type of visual sensitivity. Once again, knowing beforehand is key to coping. In some cases, you may even need to speak to the organiser to change certain elements, or even withdraw if they cannot be changed – for example if you are one of the many people on the spectrum who has epilepsy as a co-morbid (or related) medical condition. For some people, strobe lighting can cause a seizure, as can powerful spotlights or rapidly changing colours. If you have epilepsy, you would not want to speak at an event where your speech is either preceded or followed by any of these types of lighting changes.

Another consideration is the audio equipment. Sometimes a general microphone system is used which projects your voice through a small number of speakers. But sometimes (if the venue is particularly big) a formal public speaking system could be in place that booms your voice across the venue through several different speakers, with the resultant effect that your voice will echo and there will inevitably be a delay between your speaking and your words reaching the audience (as discussed above). The main things you need to be aware of are any noises coming from the system. Some public speaking systems – whatever their size – are notorious for having high frequency noises coming from them. For those of us with hypersensitive hearing, this can be torture. If you have the opportunity, ask the organiser to switch the equipment on and have someone speak into it so that you can hear if this creates the 'dreaded screech'. If you do not have the chance to do this, go to the venue prepared with some earplugs to safeguard your ears.

If you are going to be using hand-held microphones, make sure you have had the opportunity beforehand to check their sensitivity so that you can see how close (or far) you need to hold them to your mouth when you are speaking, not only to ensure that your voice projects appropriately, but also to ensure that you are not deafening your audience with inappropriately sharp 't's and 's's.

Or, if they are going to use microphones that clip onto your clothing, it is good to know this beforehand so that you can wear something appropriate. If you have hypersensitive skin, sometimes a microphone clipped to a blouse or shirt can be incredibly irritating. Therefore you need to make sure you wear something comfortable that has some sort of a lapel where the microphone can be clipped. Taking a jacket is also a good idea, so that the organiser has the opportunity to see if you are wearing something they are able to attach the microphone to, and if not they can use your jacket.

You should also be aware that some venues require the speakers to wear an earpiece. I personally find this very difficult to do, and generally have to arrange with the organiser that I either do without one or bring in one of my own. Be aware of the possibility of having to wear one, and if this could be a challenge for you, let the organiser know so that you can test the earpiece in advance.

Speaker etiquette

It is useful to know in advance exactly what is expected of you as a speaker. For example, are you going to be expected to sit on the stage with the other speakers at a speaker panel table throughout the conference? Are you expected to sit in the audience and be called up? Are you meant to be seated in a side area ready to be called up? Also, are they going to expect you to follow certain standards, such as not moving from your position while speaking, or staying on the stage the entire conference? This can be particular important for us, since we may find it extremely difficult to stay on a stage for such a long time, especially after having given a (possibly) overload creating speech, as mentioned earlier. How do they expect you to dress on the day: Is it highly formal? Do they require a dress suit or tuxedo? For ladies, do they expect you to wear an evening dress or cocktail dress? These may sound like small questions, but they are very important for you, since you do not want to arrive to find that you are getting overly stressed due to the fact that you are the only person dressed casually when everyone else is formal, for example.

I would recommend that you ensure that you are aware of the speaking order. In most cases you will be advised in advance of the order of presenters in the event, but if you have not heard anything, make certain that you find this information out. The main reason for this is that it can be extremely hard to arrive somewhere and sit waiting to be called. Consider the situation of going for an interview. You are eager, tense and yet also terrified! This is actually how most public speakers feel before being called onto the stage. If you are sitting there without knowing your 'place in the queue', every time one speaker finishes speaking, you heart is going to leap in your chest in anticipation that potentially you are next. When someone else is called, you may relax a little, but you will never get back to the point you were at when the conference began. In other words, the stress is cumulative, and if you end up being one of the last people called to speak, you may have already reached your stress overload point before you even reach the stage.

If you know that you are the fourth person to speak, while you will still be anxious and eager, you will not experience the cumulative leap in adrenaline every time one of the previous speakers finishes speaking. You will only experience it at the end of the third speaker's speech. This can make a huge difference to how well you cope.

Other essentials

Find out where the restrooms and breakaway areas are. Should you by any chance experience an overload, you do not need to be searching for a place to be able to get away from things while there are lots of other people around. You need to know where to go and how to get there.

Also make sure you know where the refreshments are either given or sold, for similar reasons. If you need to have something to drink very quickly, you do not want to discover at the last moment that there actually are not refreshments served until after the event.

It may seem that there are many practical issues for you to consider before you undertake a speaking event, but once you get into the habit of researching these sorts of things, you will find that this doesn't take as much time or effort as it may have done in the beginning. The knowledge you will have gained will make any additional effort worthwhile, and will help you to arrive at the event far more confident and reassured and able to confidently step up to deliver your speech.

In the next part of the book I talk about actually delivering your speech on the day. Before we go there, however, it is now time to refer back to Toolkit Exercise 2: Key Elements of Public Speaking (p.151) in Part 5 of the book and complete the questions for Point 2.

PART 4

Delivering Your Speech

Chapter 13

Engaging Your Audience

Public speaking can be extremely exciting for us if we are speaking about something that is of particular interest to us. We enjoy sharing knowledge, and are frequently very aware that we have more information about a topic than most people. But there are some elements of public speaking which tend to be forgotten about or put to the back of our minds when we are preparing to speak, mainly because we know that thinking about them will be challenging for us.

One of these areas is our body language and the associated eye contact that we need to use with our audience.

Your body language and mannerisms

Why is body language so important anyway, given that this tends to be an area where many of us on the autistic spectrum experience a challenge? Well, the reality is that when we give a speech, the impression that we make on the audience is based more on how we use our bodies and our voices than it is by the actual words we say. Have you heard the saying, 'It's not what you say, it's the way that you say it?' Well, this certainly is the case when it comes to speaking publicly.

In order to prepare you for the rest of this section, complete Toolkit Exercise 6: Developing Your Speaking Voice (p.168) of Part 5.

You should now be more aware of your own personal mannerisms and body language when you speak. Some of them may have come as a surprise to you. Don't be disappointed by this. Most people are not really aware of exactly how they use their bodies when they are speaking to others, so you are not alone in that. However, if you want to ensure that you make the correct impact going forward, you need to ensure that from now on you are in fact aware of how you use your body language, and that you make a conscious effort to make the right impression with your facial expression and body.

So what is the most appropriate body language for a presentation? Unfortunately (or perhaps fortunately, depending on how you look at it!), there is no standard approach. Much of it will depend on the type of event you are speaking at and the way you have determined to present yourself to the public. But here are some key recommendations:

- *Remember your smile* – It is important to smile at your audience. This helps to build a rapport with them. However, you do not want to be smiling all the way through your speech since this is not a realistic image and will be recognised as acting by your audience. It also does make a difference as to what you are speaking about. For example, if your topic of discussion is how people with disabilities can excel in the workplace, it is perfectly acceptable to smile regularly. However, if you are speaking on the topic of animal cruelty, smiling would be seen as extremely inappropriate.

- *Use your arms to provide appropriate gestures, not to fiddle* – For example, use them to emphasise size, importance, selecting an individual from the audience, and so forth. Don't be tempted to put your hands in your pockets, cross your arms or put your hands behind your back. Rather ensure that your audience can see your hands moving freely. Do not gesticulate, but use your arms reasonably.

- *Avoid fidgeting* – Sometimes this can be one of the most challenging objectives for those of us on the spectrum to achieve. Many of us go into hyperactive overdrive when we become nervous, or if we feel we are in a situation where all eyes are trained on us. One way to deal with this is through some of the coping mechanisms discussed in Chapter 4, particularly tapping. As mentioned in Toolkit Exercise 4: Changing Perceptions of Public Speaking (p.164), the mechanism of tapping can be converted by visualisation (i.e. You 'see' and 'feel' yourself tapping and experience the effects as a result). Another type of fidgeting is pacing up and down. While it is generally seen as positive to move around the stage to a certain extent (unless you are standing at a podium), pacing up and down non-stop is seen as a sign of nervousness and can be extremely distracting to the audience.

- *Avoid nervous habits* – Bad habits can include biting your nails, playing with your hair, jewellery or clothes, or even playing with a small sore or pimple on your face or neck. Try to become aware of your habits and practise avoiding them.

- *Try to practise 'speaking' with your face* – Many of us on the spectrum do find it challenging when it comes to the recognition and use of appropriate facial gestures.

Recognising bodily and facial cues from the audience

Body language is a book unto itself. What I will be focusing on are some of the most important observations for you as far as body language from your audience is concerned, and suggesting some ways to handle it.

When you become a public speaker, a very important part of being successful is to be able to recognise enough of any cues your audience is giving you to be able to understand the effect your speech is having on them so that you can make any adjustments, if necessary. For example, if you know that your audience is getting restless about you taking too long over some examples, you may decide it is better to dispense with these and move straight to the next section of your speech. Or if you pick up that your audience is struggling to keep up with you, you may decide to slow your speech down.

So what are some of the ways to identify how your audience is reacting?

Observing your audience before you speak

A very good tool for getting an idea of where your audience is and how best to present to them is to take the opportunity to observe them. If other people are speaking before you observe the way the audience are responding to them. For example, if the audience appears to be in good spirits and are laughing, then it is important to try to initially have some humour in your presentation, even if your later message is more serious. Similarly, if your audience is very serious or possibly looking slightly bored, you may need to work a bit harder to get them interested again. In other words, you will need to think about transitioning your audience from where they are to where you want them to be.

If you are the first speaker, take time to observe people during the pre-speech networking. Take the time to stand back and just view the people and how they are speaking to each other. Are they excited? Are they serious? Are they discussing certain points it will be important to cover? Are they displaying a certain outlook you need to be aware of? Also, see if you can determine the nature of your audience. In other words, are they largely business people? Therapists? Parents? Teachers? People who can identify with you personally?

Framing your speech to engage your audience

When we say that we want to engage with our audience, we are saying that we want to ensure that they go away and remember us and what we said. We need to be memorable – and memorable for the right reasons. I have already covered some of the best ways to prepare and structure your speech in order to ensure that it is most effective, and that you come across in the best way. However, here are some specific suggestions to keep in mind.

The structure of your speech

There is an optimal structure for your speech, irrespective of your audience's mood when you start your speech. This structure can be adapted to take into account what you observe of your audience before you make your speech. This comprises some key stages, as follows:

OPENING HOOK

When I speak about the opening hook, what I mean is that you need to capture your audience's interest and attention in a way that makes them curious to hear the rest of your speech. This can be done in a number of ways, but what I have found to be most effective is to use one of the following:

- *Open with a story that culminates in a key point, conflict or question* – This story should be simple and clear and yet make good use of visualisation. This is important to make sure that the people in the audience start to 'see' the story themselves as you are telling it, thereby feeling draw in. For example, rather than saying something like: 'The child was scared and didn't understand the people around her', say something along the lines of: 'The adults appeared to the child like giant aliens surrounding her and blocking any escape route she may have considered. Whenever they came near her, she felt her stomach clench and the hairs on her arms rise as her fear took hold. Their language made sense to her logically, but the meaning behind the words was beyond her reach, leaving her trembling and shaken every time someone spoke to her.' The key difference here is that you are making use of sensory imagery that other people can identify with and have possibly experienced themselves – it makes what you are describing very real to the people listening to you.

- *Open with a statement or fact that is either very striking or very concerning* – For example, 'As we sit here today, and before my speech ends, more than 100 people will be diagnosed with cancer in this state alone.' Pause for the fact to sink in. Then make a statement to open your speech, such as 'I am one of them.' Or, 'so what can we do about it?'

- *Open with a joke that has a very specific reference* – Only do this if your audience is in the right place emotionally.

POINT

Make sure that at the beginning of your speech (either as part of your opening hook or directly after this) to mention the key point of your speech. This ensures that your audience is focused on this throughout your speech.

CLARIFY

If there is a need to do so, make sure you clarify your stated point. Don't assume everyone understands your point or the terminology you use.

EXAMPLES OR STORY-TELLING

Always make use of examples or story-telling as part of your speech. People tend to remember more when things are presented to them in the form of a story. Think of the fairy tales we have remembered from early childhood. The lessons embedded in those stories are generally ones that we take to heart – because we retained them in our memories in the form of the stories themselves. Make use of this very valuable tool to ensure people remember you and what you are trying to share.

REPEAT YOUR POINT

Make sure that you end your speech by reiterating your key point in some form. You are reminding the audience of what they need to keep in mind or remember, and it will help them link it once again to any story or speech you have just made.

Engaging with your audience is about sharing your energy and passion with them. Do not hesitate to let them see your own passion and how strongly you feel about something. Use your voice and your body to let them see your energy. Look at your audience, engage with them by asking them to consider questions (even if they cannot actually answer), try to identify with them. Above all, make sure that you enjoy yourself, because this enthusiasm will flow over to your audience and they will pick up on it.

Chapter 14

The Importance of Post-Speech Socialising and Networking

You've done it! Your speech is over. The audience is clapping or otherwise acknowledging you. You are leaving the stage and making your way down to the floor. What is the first thing you want to do?

If you are a speaker on the autistic spectrum, it is highly likely that you will just want to go home and get out of the 'overload zone'. If you have not prepared effectively, you may be relying on getting some overload release, and failure to provide the opportunity for this can result in the triggering of just the overload you are trying to avoid. However, it is important for potential public speakers to be aware that it is actually very rare for your commitment to end right after your speech. For most engagements, it is expected that the speakers will, to varying extents, take part in post-speech networking.

A lot of people do not take the time to prepare for this. Socialising and networking can frequently be a key part of the public speaking event where we need to ensure that the confidence and mannerisms we have developed for our public speaking are consistent and flowing during the social interactions afterwards.

For those of us on the autistic spectrum, being asked to network straight after having given a speech can come as a shock. In general, networking is something that we find particularly challenging at any time, and if you were not aware that this was to follow straight after (or quite soon after) you have been up front giving a speech, this could be difficult to handle.

The purpose of this chapter, therefore, is twofold. First of all, it is to make you aware of what is likely to be expected of you as a public speaker when it comes to post-speech networking. Second, it aims to give you some advice as to how to network in general.

What can I expect to be asked to do after a speech?

There are a number of requirements for speakers post-event that you should be aware of, and that it is worthwhile finding out about before the event. Knowing before the event is the best way to ensure that you have prepared yourself appropriately, and to ensure that there is no risk of sudden overload. One word of warning for you: sometimes finding out what you are expected to do after the actual speech can put you off attending the event altogether! Because in most cases it involves undertaking activities that do not come naturally to us, the thought of this can often be highly stressful. Therefore, I personally find that it is best to accept speaking invitations *first* and make a formal commitment to attend. Only ask about additional commitments later on, so that by the time you hear that there is possibly some additional element that you don't particularly like the thought of, you have still made the commitment to attend. Otherwise, you run the risk of never actually participating in any of the public speaking opportunities available to you.

Here are some of the potential post-speech events that you could be asked to take part in, depending on the nature of the event and your role in it.

Book signing

If you are a published author or are speaking about one of your books, it is highly likely that you will be asked to take part in some form of book-signing after the event. In most cases, this is for a set period of time – say for a maximum of half an hour after the event. However, do be aware that organisers can sometimes treat this as an open-ended event, where a specific end of event notice is not given to the audience. This is something to avoid, because you could end up signing books and interacting with people in a single place for hours on end. If you are asked to take part in a book signing after the event, make sure that you set a time limit on this with the organiser, making it clear that you are only prepared to do it for a certain amount of time.

Business card exchange

Many events have a 30–60 minute business card exchange networking session after the event. This means is that after the formal event, drinks and snacks are made available, and speakers and audience mingle to exchange business cards and other details. This can be one of the more challenging forms of networking for us, since it involves a lot of one-to-one conversations and social chit-chat, which many of us do not find easy.

Formal networking dinner/lunch

In this type of networking, a formal dinner or lunch is arranged after the event. This is frequently less stressful for us than some of the other forms of networking, since it is centred on having a meal. If you feel that you are getting slightly overloaded, it would not be seen as unusual if you were to focus on your food, for example.

Informal networking

Informal networking is where after the formal conference, the venue is kept open for between 30 and 60 minutes, allowing people to mingle and chat. There are no formal drinks or snacks, and frequently there is no separate room in which this will take place. This can be challenging for us if we choose to take part, since it involves a lot of social interaction and informal discussions.

Q&As

Many events will end by allowing audiences to ask questions of the speakers. In this situation, it would be expected that speakers would be sitting on the stage at a speaker's table, and then questions would be raised from the floor. Be prepared for this. Ask the organiser if they intend having a Q&A session at the end, and ask them the format. That way you can make sure that you are prepared and are not overly stressed by participating.

Breakouts/workshops

Sometimes events are followed by formal breakouts or workshops for members of the audience. Although these can be interesting for the audience, they can be tiring and difficult for a person on the autistic spectrum if they are not expecting it. For this reason it is always important to ensure you know what is being done post-event.

What is networking?

A formal definition of networking obtained from the Oxford English Dictionary (2010) reads: 'Networking is a group of people who exchange information and contacts for professional or social purposes.'

Examples of networking are where people meet at a conference and end up sharing details because one person has shared that they know a potential client who is looking for a consultant to complete a piece of work that the other networker would be able to do. Another example is where two people attend a formal networking event where they end up sharing details because they discover that they have very similar backgrounds and could potentially work together on some of the new projects coming onto the market.

The importance of networking and how to ensure it is productive

Perhaps one of the most important elements of networking is that of visibility. By attending post-speech networking events at conferences and seminars, you will have the opportunity to build a presence within the public speaking arena. People will start to associate you with your area of specialisation, and when speaking opportunities arise, they will think of you. In this way, you will be raising your public speaking profile.

It is also important to understand that many people reserve their final judgment on a public speaker until they have had the opportunity to speak with them directly. Networking events are perfect for this, provided that you have prepared yourself and are able to come across as confident and relaxed as you have appeared on the stage. It is really important that your audience leaves the event speaking positively about you and about the message you have shared. The key way to make sure this happens is to take the time to be accessible to your audience for questions and general informal discussions.

Potential challenges for people on the autistic spectrum

Networking is not purely about attending post-speech events and being visible, it is about the impression you make on people you interact with when you are there, and the ultimate potential for additional speaking opportunities as a result of that interaction. In fact, this is the main reason why many of us with Asperger's groan inwardly at the thought of networking – it depends so much on the impression you make on others. Networking is an activity that is built on communication, both verbal and non-verbal, and as such it is one of those areas we possibly need to work at more than neurotypical entrepreneurs.

So why is it that people on the autistic spectrum find this activity so challenging? The most obvious answer to this is that it is an activity that is people focused. It relies on the ability to build relationships and hold informal conversations – which do not necessarily come naturally to us. We need to work on these skills, and these are activities during which we frequently find ourselves becoming overloaded. Add to that the fact that we have just been taking part in a speaking engagement, and we could find the pressures a bit too much for us, unless we have prepared.

The remainder of this chapter has been adapted from one of my other books, *An Asperger's Guide to Entrepreneurship* (Bergemann 2014).

I have been invited to speak at an event where I know I will need to network – so now what?

Okay, so we now have an idea of what networking is and why it is so important to us as public speakers. Many people on the autistic spectrum feel that taking part in post-event networking really does not help them get additional speaking invitations, since they feel overwhelmed by the requirements of networking and worry that this will make them appear stressed and unprofessional to the people who may be interested in asking them to speak. I believe that if the process of networking is simplified into some manageable steps, this will make it much easier for you to cope with and undertake, despite not being a neurotypical. What follows are some networking strategies that you can use to make the networking event less stressful and enable you to feel more in control. Let's start by breaking the networking event down into some manageable chunks.

There are three main parts to networking, together with an additional step that is specific to people on the spectrum, and each of these will have a number of steps. I will walk you through those steps as we progress and by the end of the chapter, you should be confident that you will be able to handle your next post-speech networking event. I have tried to make the format of this section more procedural, so that you can try to start thinking of networking as a process rather than a stressful encounter with others. For me, turning the networking into a visual flow-chart in my mind can certainly help me get through. This visual flow-chart is on the next page.

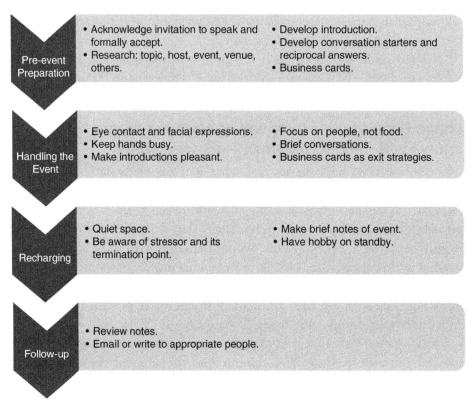

Figure 14.1 The networking flowchart

Pre-event preparation

We have discussed the process of preparing for an event and what you should do in terms of acknowledging and accepting the invitation, researching the topic, venue and so forth. However, if you know that there is going to be a networking event afterwards, there some important additional pre-event steps you need to take.

1. *Develop your introduction* – When you attend a networking event, one of the most important things for you to be comfortable doing is introducing yourself to strangers. I was once advised by someone (and I do wish I could remember who, so that I could fully acknowledge their insight!) that a trick to making a good impression in a networking session was to prepare a short introduction to yourself to use as part of your greeting. This would usually be one or two sentences. So, for example, my introduction could be, 'Hello, I'm Rosalind Bergemann, Chairman of Asperger Leaders. I mentor business leaders who are on the autistic spectrum.' As this friend

told me, the whole point of such an introduction is that the person you are addressing would then have their interest sparked enough to want to know more about you and your business.

If you have just been speaking in some sort of event ahead of the networking session, however, this really is not necessary or appropriate. If you consider that the people you are networking with would have seen you introduced on the stage already, then it is superfluous to re-introduce yourself. However, do be aware that there could be people there who were not present when you did your speech, and therefore it is worthwhile being prepared to add some additional information. If you join a group who introduce themselves to you, you should introduce yourself, for example, as follows: 'Hello, I'm Rosalind Bergemann. I spoke on the topic of Asperger's in the workplace.' It is likely at this point that you will be asked some questions about yourself, your organisation or the topic you spoke on. Therefore, I would say that it is more important for you to have thought about answers to any questions this may evoke.

2. *Develop some conversation-starter questions and your reciprocal responses* – Another thing that it is important to develop is a set of what I call opener questions. These are questions you can use to start a conversation with other people when you join a networking group. However, you will need to make sure that you not only develop some opener questions, but that you are able to carry on the reciprocal conversation. For example, a common question could be along the lines of 'So, have you worked here in Boston before?' It is hoped that the person will say yes and you can ask for more information. But they may well say, 'No, what about you?' Now the conversation has reversed and it is up to you to provide the answers and keep the listener interested. It isn't necessary to have a library of potential questions and answers. You will probably do fine with five or six standard questions that you know will need some sort of detailed response (as opposed to the 'yes' or 'no' type).

3. *Ensure you have adequate supplies of business cards* – It may sound like an obvious thing to say, but ensuring that you have adequate supplies to things like business cards is really important. There is nothing worse than realising the morning of the event that you don't have business cards and that they can only be printed in three days' time! Even if you are not a business person and want to focus strictly on public speaking, it is worthwhile having a business card, which will generally include your name and contact details, and the subject area you speak in. If you speak more generally, you can use the equivalent of your job title, which could be

'Public Speaker', or 'Published Author and Public Speaker', for example. If you do not have a business and are representing yourself as a public speaker, it is always useful to have a business card with your photograph on, since this tends to remind people where they have seen you speak.

During the event

1. *Eye contact and facial expressions* – I don't need to tell you that this is an area where a large percentage of us tend to have some challenges. Again, I am not going to go into too much detail on this. Keep in mind that you should have a smile on your face when you introduce yourself, and that you should keep regular eye contact. Beware, though, of ending up staring at people. Regular eye contact means that you occasionally look away (for example, at your glass or anything in your hand), but return your eyes to theirs when they speak. It is always a good idea, if this is an area you are challenged with, to practise in front of a mirror or ask someone that you trust to have a practice networking session with you so that they can give you some feedback. The most important requirements are that you smile, introduce yourself and offer your hand for a handshake. Firm, brief handshakes are best – avoid limp, cripplingly tight or 'shoulder breaking' handshakes. Just one or two firm shakes and then let go.

2. *Keep your hands busy* – Keep something in your hands. I do not mean something large or unwieldy. It needs to be something relatively inconspicuous and comfortable for you to hold while you carry on a conversation with someone. Examples here would be a teacup, a wine glass, a plate with a couple of nibbles on it (see my note later on about eating while networking), a business card holder or a brochure. It needs to be something that you are able to hold comfortably while shaking hands with a person you are being introduced to, so large books, multiple papers or large plates of food would be inappropriate. Most people don't really know what to do with their hands if they are just standing around. People can end up folding their arms (a very defensive gesture), putting their hands in their pockets (seen as a scruffy or careless look) or even just clasping their hands together in front of them (often seen as an unconfident look). In addition, some of us on the spectrum have a tendency to stim when we are nervous, which means that we may make repetitive movements with our arms or hands, such as drumming our fingers on our legs, swinging our arms slightly or even what they call flapping. Most of the time we don't even realise we are doing this.

Sometimes this can be highly distracting for other people, and will put people off coming to speak with us. Holding something comfortably in your hand will make you look more relaxed and hence more approachable.

3. *Make introductions pleasant* – Again, this may seem obvious, but is not always straightforward. Some essentials for you to keep in mind when making introductions are:

    a. When joining a group, never interrupt someone speaking or just join the conversation. Always wait for an appropriate moment and then introduce yourself before adding any comments. The only exception to this general rule is when you are finding it challenging to find a point of entrance into the conversation. Sometimes you need to join by acknowledging the comment of another person before introducing yourself. For example, making the comment, 'I couldn't agree more with you. My name is Rosalind Bergemann, by the way. I spoke earlier on a similar topic.' In this way you have gently interrupted the discussion to get into the conversation.

    b. Make sure that you give your attention to all participants in the conversation at appropriate times, not just one.

4. *Focus on people, not food* – Here is another consideration which may seem obvious but which frequently isn't considered by networkers. If you are attending an event where there are light refreshments during networking, make sure that you are not focusing more on the food than you are on the networking. Again, this is not a comment that I would make exclusively to people on the spectrum. Neurotypicals can be just as naive about this as anyone. Think about it. People trying to have a conversation with someone really do not enjoy watching them eat while they speak to them. Also, beware of over-eating. You are there to network, not for a meal.

    Use your plate as your item to keep in your hand, and rather focus on speaking to people than specifically eating anything. You could discretely 'nibble' at your food, possibly when other people in the networking group are speaking to each other, rather than to you. Above all else, make sure that you avoid shaking hands after having handled food without wiping your hand on your napkin first.

5. *Hold brief conversations* – Networking works by allowing people the opportunity to meet new people and exchange details. What you don't need to do is to turn the event into a minor meeting by making your conversations too long. As a guideline, you should be speaking to individuals (or a small group of people) for no more than 15 minutes.

After that time you need to move on to someone else by utilising your exit strategy, as described below.

6. *Exchange business cards as an exit strategy* – Once you have completed your conversation, it is important that you exit from the conversation in an efficient and amiable manner. The best way to do this is to initiate the exchange of business cards, because most people recognise this as a signal that the conversation has come to a close. Find an appropriate time in the conversation to break eye contact, look into your purse or look to your pocket to retrieve a business card, and say something like, 'Let me give you one of my business cards…' At this point the person or people you are speaking to will generally reciprocate by offering you theirs. End the conversation by saying that it was nice speaking with them.

Follow-up: Email or write to people who shared their business cards

In building a public speaking profile, it is very important to acknowledge people who have shared their details or business cards with you. This helps to reinforce your conversations, imbed their impression of you as a speaker, and provide them with the impression that you are the type of person who cares about the people you speak to and who can be relied on. Although you may wonder why this is important, frequently in deciding who to invite to speak at an event, organisers will consider who can be depended on to arrive after having given an initial agreement to take part. They will also call to mind people who have been social enough to acknowledge the networking conversation. So, as you can see, follow-up is an important part of networking itself.

Once you have decided who you want to make contact with, send them a note within the first few days of the event to make contact and thank them for the time they spent speaking with you. If you have a street address for the person, try to send this as a hard-copy letter, since this tends to make more of an impression and is more likely to be read than an email. However, if you do only have an email address, do still send your email.

Your initial communication should be brief, just thanking them for their time and sharing that it was good to meet them. Tell them you enjoyed speaking with them and invite them to contact you should they ever have need of a speaker in that particular area of interest, or if they feel you could make a contribution in any other area.

While you may feel that your particular area of public speaking is quite niche and the above comments may be inappropriate, it is important to remember that many people may see your contribution from a completely different perspective and recognise that you have a lot to share in another related area. If you tell people you are only prepared to speak on a very specific topic, you may give the impression that you are not serious about sharing publicly, which will put potential organisers off.

If someone does contact you about potentially speaking in a different subject area than the one you are used to speaking in, do ask the organiser in what way they feel that you would add value to the event. What they tell you could give you great insight into additional impacts your speaking is having that you may not have considered. Never argue with them if this is something you do not agree with. If you feel that this would not be a good match for you, just thank them for the invitation and decline, saying that unfortunately you will not be able to attend. You do not need to explain your reasons for this decision. By declining in this way, you will leave the door open for other opportunities from that person in the future.

Some basic elements of body language to consider

Finally, I would like to briefly cover a very important consideration when it comes to post-speech networking – body language. Reading body language for those of us who have an autistic spectrum disorder can sometimes be extremely challenging. It can be an area of weakness for us, and although we may have sufficiently mastered this to operate well within the predominantly neurotypical world, the stresses of attending a post speech networking event can sometimes make our self-conditioning go out the window, as they say.

As I have mentioned, this is an area where a significant amount of learning can be shared – as is the topic of networking as a whole. I am going to mention a few body language 'markers' that you should be aware of in the networking environment.

Negative body language

When you are speaking with someone, you need to be aware of when they start to display negative body language, because this could very well be their way of trying to tell you that they are tired of the conversation or do not want to continue to network with you right then. If you ignore the body signals people are giving you, people can become irritated, annoyed or even downright angry with you, believing that you are ignoring the signals on purpose.

So what are some of the most common negative body cues that you should try to keep alert for?

LOSS OF EYE CONTACT

Loss of eye contact from a neurotypical always indicates a negative signal if they had been having reasonable eye contact with you before. As people on the spectrum, we are sometimes less aware of this being an issue because we have to force ourselves to remember to make eye contact. Therefore, someone not making eye contact actually feels more genuine to us! However, do keep in mind that failure to make good eye contact is not the exclusive realm of people on the spectrum. Sometimes neurotypicals who are introverted or shy can be just as eye-elusive. What you need to look out for is a *change* in eye contact from eye contact to lack of eye contact. This is the negative signal. So, for example, you could be having a conversation with someone who is initially looking at you most of the time (good eye contact). After a while you notice that he is starting to watch other people walking past or to stare at the ground or some other object rather than looking at you (distraction). You continue talking, but then notice that the person is hardly making eye contact at all and is looking around or making eye contact with other people outside your conversation group (negative eye contact).

FOLDING ARMS

When people suddenly fold their arms across their chests and stop talking as much as they were, this is a sign that the person is not comfortable talking to you – for whatever reason.

Again, you need to be aware that this does not mean every occurrence of folding arms is a negative one. You need to take the context into account. Say, for example, that you are standing outside, networking. The woman you are talking to is wearing a light blouse and no jacket. As you talk, the weather takes a turn for the worse and the wind picks up. If the woman folds her arms across her chest at this time, it is in all likelihood because she is cold, not because she is uncomfortable speaking with you.

What you should look for if you see the person fold their arms over their chest are any of the following additional signs:

- Have they stopped conversing as much as they were?

- Are they leaning away from you, or turning their body away from you?

- Are they frowning?

- Are they sighing or losing eye contact?

If you notice any of these, take it that this is a negative body signal and move on.

TURNING AWAY OF THE BODY

Another negative body signal is when people start to turn their bodies away from you so that they are not facing you properly. This can sometimes be easy to miss if you are concentrating on having a good conversation.

The best way to check is to glance at the person's shoulders. Are they facing towards you or in your direction, or is one shoulder behind the other – almost as if the person is beginning to turn away from you in slow motion? This can either be the person indicating to you that they want to move on or that they want to speak with someone else. Again, take context into account. If the person is likely to be turning because the sun is in their eyes, this is not the same situation.

INTRUSION OF PERSONAL SPACE

Although this may not sound like a negative, something that can go wrong at a networking event is that a person could try to become personal when you are trying to be professional. We need to be aware that sometimes we may not pick up when someone starts flirting with us. The best way to avoid this is to keep the concept of personal space in mind.

Most of us on the spectrum are not comfortable with people being too close to us – it just comes with the territory. Many of us have families or careers and so have had to learn to overcome our aversion and to just cope with the feelings. Because of this, we may actually have made ourselves insensitive to people stepping into our personal space inappropriately, and rather than reacting as a neurotypical would, we automatically tell ourselves that we are being oversensitive and that we need to just put up with the negative feelings.

I recommend that you try to keep the following in mind to help you determine if you have someone possibly trying to get overly personal with you:

- The definition of personal space will vary depending on where in the world you live. In most western cultures, personal space is seen as the space surrounding you up to an arm's length or about half a metre. People coming within this in a professional setting such as a networking event are violating your personal place.

- Be aware of your environment. Could the person be moving closer to you because it is very noisy and they are trying to hear you? If so, do you need to speak louder so that they can move back?

- Does the person possibly have a hearing difficulty? Have you noticed if they move closer to everyone they speak to?

- Does the person appear to be smiling a lot, and looking up at you from a lowered head (if she is a woman) or down at you with eyes that are not wide open (if you are a woman)? This could indicate that they are attracted to you and are speaking to you personally rather than professionally.

- If you move away from them, do they move forward again? This could indicate that they are violating your personal space intentionally.

- Are they looking at your body sometimes rather than making eye contact?

If you are at a networking event and you are not interested in any personal relationships developing as a result (which I am sure you are not!), then now is the time to make a professional exit and move on. Do *not* offer them your business card, but rather say that you need to mingle some more, and that it was good speaking to them. Don't wait for a response, but move on immediately.

While the chapter has ended by discussing some of the smaller challenges of networking and socialising, do keep in mind that this is an important area of your development as a public speaker as well as of your personal growth. As you continue to network, some of the strategies I have highlighted for you will become second nature to you, and the process will – believe it or not – become easier. You may never become completely comfortable with the process of networking – many of us never do – but none of the people you network with will ever be able to tell that, and the success you have in your speaking as a result of your contacts will certainly make you feel that it was worth all the effort you have put into it.

Chapter 15

Managing Sensory Overload Issues after Your Speech

For those of us on the spectrum, an area that we need to be aware of when undertaking any public speaking or post-speech socialising event is the potential for us to experience some sort of sensory overload. This is not something that we need to feel concerned or embarrassed about. I know many people who are ashamed of the way that sensory overload can affect them. I prefer to think of this as just part of who I am, the same way that someone who is allergic to certain foods learns how to deal with that, or someone who has dyslexia learns how to deal with the challenges their own developmental condition presents them with. Sensory overload is not a short-fall on our side. It is part of the way we are, and rather than seeing it as a weakness, I prefer to think about our ability to developing coping strategies as being a personal strength. People who have never had to deal with an overload have never had to learn to cope with overwhelming issues as a regular occurrence and hence may not be able to handle one if they ever get to experience it. We, on the other hand, are experts at coping. So keep that in mind while you work through this chapter – focus on your strength and not what you perceive to be your weakness.

Overload issues that may arise during post-speech networking

Perhaps the best way to start thinking about the coping strategies you are going to use in your post-speech socialising environment is to initially think about what potential overload issues could arise – if any arise at all.

As I have mentioned previously, one of the ways in which we tend to recuperate from a stressful event involving other people is to get some time alone. This is something I refer to as 'recharging', and I will discuss recharging after the event is completely over a little later in the chapter. However, one of the biggest causes of sensory overload can be when you need to have a recharging break and are unable to do so. What happens is that you end up getting tense because you cannot relieve your stressor, then end up getting tense because you are getting tense. As you can imagine, this becomes a vicious circle of tension that can ultimately trigger either an overload or some type of issue with any co-morbid conditions you may have (such as an asthma attack).

One of the best ways to avoid this type of overload is to be prepared for the fact that you are going to be required to continue to be people-facing post-speech, and therefore not expect to be able to recharge until later on. If you are not anticipating the opportunity to recharge at this time, it will not be stressful for you when you have to stay in that environment.

However, even if we know that we are going to be required to stay in the 'uncomfortable' environment post-speech, that doesn't always help us to eliminate the build up of tension that has occurred during the event so far. For this reason, it is always good to have a back-up coping strategy. This is why I recommended that it is important to ensure you know where the toilets and restrooms are at a venue as part of your preparation. If you find that you are stressed at the end of your speech and you need some recharging time, excuse yourself from the event and go to the bathroom. I am the first to say that closing myself in the bathroom has worked wonders for me at certain times.

Another method that I have found useful if I am required to stay behind for things such as Q&As is to doodle. Yes, that's right – doodle! If you are asked to stay behind after your speech to sit at a speakers' table and take questions from the audience, if at all possible make sure that there are some sort of notepads available on the table. You are entitled to ask the organiser to arrange this for you. Then, if at any point you feel particularly overloaded, drop your head and spend some time focusing on doodling. I suggest doodling as opposed to writing because doodling tends to be more creative and therefore requires you to use a different part of your brain to the one that is likely to be going into 'overload freeze'. However, where you can, do try to ensure that you do occasionally lift your head and look at your audience, or it may appear that you are uninterested in the event or disengaged, and this leaves a negative impression with an audience. I recommend that you practise the unique art of 'doodley-attention' (my own word!). This is where you doodle or draw on a notepad while still maintaining reasonable eye contact with the audience, hence showing that you are paying attention to them. As a result, as far as the doodling goes, you are drawing more by feel than by sight. This shift in concentration will help you to lower your overload levels by focusing your attention on undertaking what is usually a slightly challenging (or at least interesting!) task.

Another concern can be that we could start to get overloaded and switch off. If you find that this is happening in your post-speech networking, do know that it is perfectly acceptable for you to excuse yourself and leave, saying that you have had a long day and need to retire.

Recharging at home

Most people would assume that once you have left the venue, that is all you need to worry about. Actually, I would disagree on that point, and am going to raise a couple of points that I think are important for you to have considered beforehand.

In order for us to regain our composure and effectively recover from this public speaking event, it is generally a good idea for you to build into your schedule some time after the event to recharge. Never make the mistake of scheduling another meeting or important activity after your speech other than the potential networking events we have discussed. In reality, you are highly unlikely to be up to facing it and if you do, you are likely to experience additional stress.

What follows are some suggestions on how to prepare for a recharging session in the best way.

1. *Have a quiet space prepared or made ready for you* – If you are speaking publicly, try to ensure beforehand that you have an 'escape area' prepared for you at home afterwards. If you are not going straight home after the event, this can be an office or meeting room at your workplace that you should ensure you formally book. If you are going home straight afterwards and have a family, make certain that they are aware that you need some alone time and are not to be disturbed for an agreed period of time.

2. *Be aware of the stressor, but know it is controllable* – Be aware that speaking publicly may be a stressors for you, and accept that this is not a fault on your side: it is just part of who you are. It doesn't help to try to imagine that you are not going to be affected by this, or condone yourself for your perceived failures in your social skills. Instead, know it *will* be challenging, but be confident that you have coping strategies in place and that you are the type of person who can overcome a challenge successfully. At the end of the event, be reassured that the stressor is over and therefore you are able to move on from this. Congratulate yourself on a job well

done. We know it isn't easy, but you faced it and made it through. Using the strategies in this chapter, it will not be as stressful as it might have previously been.

3. *Consider making brief notes* – When you are in your quiet place, you may want to think about taking some time to make brief notes about the event and any people you have met during the post-speech networking. You will be surprised at how quickly a person can forget important information when it has been obtained in a difficult or uncomfortable environment.

4. *Have a hobby on standby* – There is absolutely no better way to unwind and clear your mind of any residual negative effects of a stressor than to make use of a special hobby, especially for most of us on the spectrum. Things like reading, building things, computer games, pets or studying – whatever your special interest is – they are all valuable to us because we enjoy doing them and we relax as we do them. I have sometimes used the thought of one of my hobbies as a motivator to get me through a particularly intense networking session, and I have found this a very strong form of encouragement for me. Think about how you can use your own hobbies and areas of special interest to work for you in this area.

I like to spend some time remembering the positive elements of the event. It is extremely easy to focus on or recall any negative feelings or occurrences you experienced at the event, but it is not so easy to bring to mind all the positives unless you train yourself to do so. Make sure that you remember, and wherever possible write down, the positive experience(s) you had. This ensures that the next time you are invited to speak, it is these positive experiences that come to mind first and not any negative ones. If you do experience negative feelings or thoughts when you are asked to speak again, make the determined effort to pull to mind all those positives you articulated. This will ensure that going forward, the thought of speaking publicly will fill you with excitement and not dread.

Now that you have completed the majority of the book, do take the time to refer back to Toolkit Exercise 2 in Part 5 of the book and complete the questions for Point 3. This should give you an idea of how your thinking has progressed and highlight any areas of your own personal development that have improved or still need to be worked on.

Conclusion

For many of you considering speaking publicly – for work, on behalf of an organisation or as part of your own personal career – even opening this book may have been an extreme challenge. Much as some people like to boast, public speaking does not come naturally to anyone – it is a skill that we have to learn and develop in order to become our best. I hope that as you have gone through this book you have seen that you are by no means alone if you have been fearful of standing up and speaking. I would say that *everyone* undertaking public speaking is fearful at some time. The only difference is that as time goes on and people prepare better, that fear become less and less. Key to reducing the fear is preparation, and I hope the exercises in this book have helped you to build your confidence as a public speaker.

I also hope that this book has helped to dispel any myths that we, as people on the autistic spectrum, cannot be highly charismatic speakers. The toolkit exercises have helped you to see that you, too, can be one of them by providing you with the tools and guidance you need.

I encourage you to keep the principles of SPEAK in mind whenever you are considering, preparing for or actually speaking, and encourage yourself that you are able to meet your audience's expectations. You now have a far better understanding of yourself as an individual as far as public speaking is concerned. Public speaking is something you will develop and improve in as you go. It is one of those areas where the saying 'practice makes perfect' is true! But the best form of practice is not standing in front of a mirror – it is going out and making those presentations and learning from each one!

I salute you in your new public speaking endeavours and look forward to seeing some new speakers from the autistic spectrum shining in the public speaking arena!

Part 5 contains a number of toolkits and exercises which are available to be downloaded from www.jkp.com/UK/an-asperger-s-guide-to-public-speaking.html.

Practical Tools for People on the Autistic Spectrum Preparing for Public Speaking

TOOLKIT EXERCISE 1

YOUR INITIAL THOUGHTS

For each of the following questions, select an answer that feels most appropriate for you. It could well be that there is no answer which completely corresponds with your observations. In this case, try to select the closest answer where appropriate, leaving the 'I do not know' option as a last resort. The questionnaire aims at asking you how you currently present. If you have not started public speaking yet, try to complete the questionnaire to say what you think you would do when you start speaking.

Question	Answer a	Answer b	Answer c	Answer d
1. How do you feel when you think about going to a public speaking event?	It makes me feel panicky and nervous.	I like the thought of doing it, but it makes me nervous when I think about actually standing up and speaking.	I really want to do it and think it will be exciting.	I don't know.
2. How much do you practise?	I don't spend more than an hour practising.	I can spend several days practising – at least 20 hours.	I spend about 4–5 hours practising.	I don't practise.
3. How long are your speeches in general when typed up?	My speeches tend to be very detailed so are very long – about 10 pages or more.	My speeches are generally about 5–6 pages long.	My speeches are about 2 to 3 pages long.	My speeches tend to be 1–2 pages long.
4. How do you prefer to present?	I prefer to present behind a podium.	I prefer to present on an open stage.	I have no particular preference.	I don't know.

Question	Answer a	Answer b	Answer c	Answer d
5. Do you research your audience at all?	I have a look at the number of people attending.	I look at what type of event it is – that tells me what I need to know.	I research what type of event it is, as well as the types of people invited.	No.
6. Do you have a strategy to deal with your pre-speech nerves?	I don't think I need one.	I deal with it on the day.	Yes.	No.
7. What do you do after your speech?	I leave immediately.	I stay around for any post-speech drinks and eats.	I stay to network with other speakers and the audience.	I don't know.
8. How do you deal with any overload issues arising?	I leave.	I would make use of my normal coping strategies.	I have reviewed my coping strategies and have specific strategies for this situation.	I hadn't thought about it.

Now that you have completed this exercise, score your answers as follows:

All answers in the Answer a column score **1**.

All answers in the Answer b column score **2**.

All answers in the Answer c column score **3**.

All answers in the Answer 4 column score **0**.

Score below 13:

The thought of presenting makes you nervous, and you potentially do not undertake enough preparation for the event. You should find all of the book useful.

Score between 13 and 19:

One of the areas you can develop is to optimise the format of your speech and the way it is presented. Parts 2 and 4, as well as Chapters 11 and 12 in Part 3 could be particularly useful for you, together with the associated Toolkit Exercises.

Score over 19:

You already have developed a good approach to public speaking. However, you may still need to focus on tailoring your speech to your audience as well as making sure that you make good use of networking opportunities after the event. While all the material may provide some additional insights, it is likely that Parts 2 and 4 may be most beneficial for you.

KEY ELEMENTS OF PUBLIC SPEAKING

In Chapter 2 of the book, you were introduced to the five key elements of public speaking through which I consider people make their impact when they speak publicly (known by the acronym SPEAK). These five areas are:

- *Self-knowledge* – Having an understanding of your own personal speaking style, areas that make you unique, and a full understanding of and mechanism to apply any necessary coping or adjustment techniques that are all your own.

- *Passion and charisma* – Feeling impassioned about what you are speaking about and being able to captivate your audience and inspire them in some way using this passion.

- *Empathy* – Speaking to an audience and being able to understand and/or perceive how they are reacting to your message.

- *Authority* – Speaking about your topic with confidence and in such a way that the audience trusts you and hence sees you as an authority on the topic.

- *Knowledge* – Having the necessary facts and information covering the topic being discussed, over and above the level of knowledge of the average member of the audience.

Take a few minutes now to consider either your current public speaking style if you already speak publicly, or what you believe your style will be if you have yet to start. Consider what may apply to you, where you think you may have particular strengths, or where you feel you need to develop further. It is important that you complete this exercise without asking for any additional observations from anyone else. This is a record of how you perceive your own speaking style ahead of any development exercises in this book. Now take the time to populate the table on the following pages for each of the key areas given under the section 'Now'. Note that it is important to complete each box in the grid, even if you make the statement 'I don't know'.

Key Areas of Impact		How do I generally handle this area of impact?	What are my strengths?	Where must I develop?
Self-knowledge	Now			
	Point 1			
	Point 2			
	Point 3			
Passion and charisma	Now			
	Point 1			
	Point 2			
	Point 3			

Empathy			
Now			
Point 1			
Point 2			
Point 3			
Authority			
Now			
Point 1			
Point 2			
Point 3			

Key Areas of Impact	How do I generally handle this area of impact?	What are my strengths?	Where must I develop?
Knowledge	Now		
	Point 1		
	Point 2		
	Point 3		

Your answers will give you an initial idea of where you think you need to get additional input from this book, and will also provide a foundation to build on as you learn new techniques and tools. At various points in the book I will challenge you to review your original answers and see if they have changed in any way.

TOOLKIT EXERCISE 3

EARLY COPING STRATEGIES

In Chapter 4 we started to talk about how best to develop some early coping strategies for public speaking if there is the potential that you may find this challenging. Part of determining any coping strategy for you is to identify what challenges you may face and how you may react to them.

The following exercise is split into two parts. The first part is going to challenge you to think about any key individual behaviour that you may have that you consider to be either inappropriate or something you would prefer an audience not to see because it is too personal. Keep in mind as you do this exercise that we are not looking for faults here. We are trying to make you think of any possible ways you could react so that these reactions are fresh in your mind as you go to further toolkits later in the chapter. Part 2 of the exercise will ask you to consider what coping strategies you currently have in place for those behaviours.

Part 1: Your individual behaviours

Instructions

The following table show some of the more common issues experienced by those of us on the autistic spectrum and allows you to indicate the degree to which these were representative of your behaviour while undertaking a stressful activity.

	Does not apply	Mild to irregular	Quite often	Regularly	Almost all the time	Key problem area
Aggression/overly assertive						
Isolating oneself						
Anxiety						
Depression						
Tantrums/outbursts						

cont.

	Does not apply	Mild to irregular	Quite often	Regularly	Almost all the time	Key problem area
Inability or difficulty making friends						
Problems with teamwork						
Problems with conversations (inappropriate comments, speaking too fast/slow, interrupting others, going off topic)						
Rituals or compulsory behaviours						
Specialist interest being too focused						
Difficulties understanding other people's thoughts or reactions (mindblindness)						
Sensory hypersensitivities						
Poor co-ordination and/or balance						
Stimming behaviour						
Problems interpreting instructions (taking things too literally)						
Very blunt/matter of fact with opinions						
Problems with personal body language (lack of or inappropriate facial expressions, gestures or actions, inappropriate stimming)						
Problems interpreting body language in others						
Problems with eye contact						
Problems with proximity/personal space						
Hypervigilance						
Inability to focus on a task due to distractions						
Getting too caught up in the details of an assignment without being able to see the overview (e.g. writing a detailed essay but not being able to summarise it appropriately)						
Perfectionism (struggling to leave tasks until they are perfect)						
Difficulty with verbal directions or instructions						

	Does not apply	Mild to irregular	Quite often	Regularly	Almost all the time	Key problem area
Dependent on instructions; not being proactive						
Insistence of doing things 'your way' and no other						
Problems multitasking						
Problems delegating						
Sensory overload						
Shutdown or deliberate isolation						
Others (detail)						

Part 2: Your current coping strategies

Having thought about your key behavioural indicators, isolate those behaviours you have indicated as occurring 'Quite often' or more. Think about how you have managed them over time, detailing any coping strategies that you have developed.

	How have I managed this in the past? Do I have a formal coping strategy I use?
Aggression/overly assertive	

cont.

	How have I managed this in the past? Do I have a formal coping strategy I use?
Isolating oneself	
Anxiety	
Depression	
Tantrums/outbursts	
Inability or difficulty making friends	

Problems with teamwork	
Problems with conversations (inappropriate comments, speaking too fast/slow, interrupting others, going off topic)	
Rituals or compulsory behaviours	
Specialist interest being focal	
Difficulties understanding other people's thoughts or reactions (mindblindness)	
Sensory hypersensitivities	

cont.

	How have I managed this in the past? Do I have a formal coping strategy I use?
Poor co-ordination and/or balance	
Stimming behaviour	
Problems interpreting instructions (taking things too literally)	
Very blunt/matter of fact with opinions	
Problems with personal body language (lack of or inappropriate facial expressions, gestures or actions, inappropriate stimming)	

Problems interpreting body language in others	
Hypervigilance	
Problems with eye contact	
Problems with proximity/ personal space	
Inability to focus on a task due to distractions	
Getting too caught up in the details of an assignment without being able to see the overview (e.g. writing a detailed essay but not being able to summarise it appropriately)	

cont.

	How have I managed this in the past? Do I have a formal coping strategy I use?
Perfectionism (struggling to leave tasks until they are perfect)	
Difficulty with verbal directions or instructions	
Dependent on instructions; not being proactive	
Insistence of doing things 'your way' and no other	
Problems multitasking	

Problems delegating	
Sensory overload	
Shutdown or deliberate isolation	
Others (detail)	

CHANGING PERCEPTIONS OF PUBLIC SPEAKING

In Chapter 4 we talked about some generic coping strategies that you can use to overcome your social communication or public speaking anxiety. The following toolkit is going to walk you through the process of changing your perceptions of public speaking from a stressor to an opportunity, so that you do not have the negative physical reactions to stress that you may currently be experiencing. The exercises that follow are based on a combination of what are known as cognitive behavioural therapy and neurolinguistic programming techniques. These may sound highly technical, but effectively what these represent are psychological tools to help you adjust your thinking to something that is more effective for you.

A large part of the exercise here involves visualisation, and I am aware that for some people this can be difficult to do. For that reason I have split this exercise into two – one for people who are able to undertake visualisation exercises, and one for people who need to have more a physical input. Note that you will only need to complete one of the exercises, depending on what is best for you. If you do not know whether or not you are able to undertake visualisation exercises, I recommend that you start with Part 1: Understanding your current situation using visualisation. If you find that you are not able to complete the visualisation exercise, then move to Part 2: Understanding your current situation without visualisation.

Part 1: Understanding your current reactions using visualisation

Instructions

Find a quiet place where you can isolate yourself and sit down undisturbed. It is very important that you follow the steps in sequence, so read through them first to familiarise yourself with what you need to do. As you imagine each of the steps listed below, try to make them as real as possible. For example, when you are asked to imagine preparing for and then going to your public speaking event, do not just picture yourself getting dressed, then suddenly being at the event. Imagine the actual steps involved: getting dressed, doing your tie/make-up, preparing your notes, getting into your car, driving to the venue, and so on.

- Close your eyes and imagine you are doing your last minute preparation for your public speaking event. Try to allow yourself to experience any emotions you may be feeling, such as nervousness about the time running out to prepare, worry that your speech is too long, anger at yourself for not preparing more, and so forth.

- Next imagine getting dressed and prepared to go to the event. Again, allow yourself to feel whatever your body is telling you. Are you starting to feel knots in your stomach? Are the muscles in your neck tensing up? Spend some time acknowledging your feelings.

- Next, imagine going to your public speaking event and preparing to go on stage. Once again, make sure you take the time to notice what you are feeling, what you are experiencing, what your body is telling you.

While you are experiencing the above reactions, make a conscious effort to change the negative thinking or feelings you are experiencing by replacing them with something positive. So, for example, you could have been feeling worried that people are going to think your speech is not professional enough. Change that thinking now to picture your audience nodding in appreciation, or leaning forward eagerly. If one of your concerns is that you will stumble on the stage, picture yourself striding confidently across the stage with invisible barriers ensuring you have a handhold. Your imagination is a powerful thing, and starting to visualise something positive – or even funny – rather than something negative, will ultimately begin to influence how your body perceives what was previously seen as a threat.

I personally tend to see my life visually as a movie, so if I am trying to envisage something changing, I sometimes see my character played by someone I really admire, and frequently I will add music to my event, hearing anticipatory music as I approach the venue, and trumpets of excitement as I get up to go to the stage.

Experiment with what works for you. Remember this is something you may need to do a number of times to ensure your feelings continue to pick on your positive thoughts.

Part 2: Understanding your current reactions without using visualisation

Instructions

Make arrangements to undertake a small public speaking event, such as speaking to your staff or making a small speech to a group of friends. Rather than imagining each of the steps listed below, try to make a mental record of what happens as you actually experience them. For example, when you are asked to acknowledge what is happening while you are preparing for and then going to your public speaking event, do your best to acknowledge all your feelings, what your body is telling you, as well as what you may realise to be the reasons (don't worry if you do not know the reason).

- During your last minute preparation for your public speaking event try to allow yourself to experience any emotions you may be feeling, such as nervousness about the time running out to prepare, worry that your speech is too long, anger at yourself for not preparing more, and so forth. Try to make either a mental record of what you are feeling, or a brief written note somewhere.

- Do the same while getting dressed and prepared to go to the event. Again, allow yourself to feel whatever your body is telling you. Are you starting to feel knots in your stomach? Are the muscles in your neck tensing up? Spend some time acknowledging your feelings.

- Next, make a note of your reactions while going to your public speaking event and preparing to go on stage. Once again, make sure you take the time to notice what you are feeling, what you are experiencing, what your body is telling you.

While you are experiencing the above reactions, make a conscious effort to change the negative thinking or feelings you are experiencing by replacing them with positive ones. So, for example, you could have been feeling worried that people are going to think your speech is not professional enough. Change that thinking now to picture your audience nodding in appreciation, or leaning forward eagerly. If one of your concerns is that you will stumble on the stage, picture yourself striding confidently across the stage with invisible barriers ensuring you have a handhold. Your imagination is a powerful thing, and starting to visualise something positive – or even funny – rather than something negative, will ultimately begin to influence how your body perceives what was previously seen as a threat.

I personally tend to see my life visually as a movie, so if I am trying to envisage something changing, I sometimes see my character played by someone I really admire, and frequently I will add music to my event, hearing anticipatory music as I approach the venue, and trumpets of excitement as I get up to go to the stage.

Experiment with what works for you. Remember this is something you may need to do a number of times to ensure your feelings continue to pick up on your positive thoughts.

TOOLKIT EXERCISE 5

DEVELOPING YOUR PUBLIC SPEAKING PERSONA

In order to prepare for your public speaking career, you need to develop your public speaking persona, as discussed in Chapter 5. A key part in doing so is to understand your personal purpose when it comes to speaking.

In order to better understand your personal purpose in the public speaking sense, take some time now to complete the following table which will walk you through some considerations of what is important to you in your speaking.

Question	Your response
What is important about public speaking for me as a person? Why do I want to do it?	
What do I find exciting about the prospect of speaking publicly?	
What is my key message that I want to share with people in general (e.g. people on the spectrum have great skills)?	
What is important about my message to the audience as a whole (e.g. it is a unique insight)?	
What value can my message give to the audience (e.g. it will inspire people)?	

Keep your above responses in mind when you consider what it is about you that makes your public speaking persona unique.

DEVELOPING YOUR SPEAKING VOICE

In order to prepare for your public speaking career, it is very valuable to be aware of your current speaking and presenting style. This toolkit offers you some strategies to determine what are some of your key mannerisms and distinctive speaking style.

The first step in determining your speaking style is through personal observation of how you think you present yourself. Frequently, the way we perceive ourselves to be presenting can turn out to be very different from the actual way we do present. Part 1, which is the first of a couple of exercises, will help you formally identify your *expected* speaking style. Please note that you will require a notebook to record your observations.

Part 1: Mannerisms at rest

Find a full length mirror and position yourself where you have clear sight of your full body. Stand for a couple of minutes just taking in how you appear to stand when you are at rest. For example, do you stand in a way that appears to be completely relaxed, or do you 'strum' your fingers on your thigh as you stand still? Do you tap your heels? Do you tend to cross your hands in front of your hips, or cross your ankles?

Now complete the following table. Remember to be as observant and as honest as you can. Try to allow yourself to be natural – what you are *usually* like. You don't want to try to modify your behaviour in any way right now.

Do you display the following when at rest?	Give details
Clenching of fists	
Shaking or rubbing of hands	
Tapping fingers on thigh	
Swinging arms	
Crossing arms	
Clutching hands together in front of you	
Moving legs (e.g. bending knees and straightening)	
Rubbing chin	

Do you display the following when at rest?	Give details
Playing with tie/jewellery/clothing	
Playing with hair	
Jingling coins in your pocket	
Playing with your glasses, or constantly putting them on and taking them off	
Fiddling with objects such as pens, highlighters, etc.	
Other:	

Part 2: Mannerisms while speaking

Organise for a friend or colleague to make a video recording of you making a short speech, either an actual event or one you have put together for the purposes of this exercise. Make sure that it lasts at least 20 minutes. If this is something you are doing just for the purposes of this exercise, try to make the venue and audience as realistic as possible so that you can experience the same sort of stressors you would if you were actually speaking at an event.

Once you have completed your speech, go through the video recording and make a note of your body language and mannerisms again in the table that follows.

Do you display the following when speaking to an audience?	Give details
Clenching of fists	
Shaking or rubbing of hands	
Tapping fingers on thigh	
Swinging arms	
Crossing arms	
Clutching hands together in front of you	
Moving legs (e.g. bending knees and straightening)	
Rubbing chin	
Playing with tie/jewellery/clothing	

cont.

Do you display the following when speaking to an audience?	Give details
Playing with hair	
Jingling coins in your pocket	
Playing with your glasses, or constantly putting them on and taking them off	
Fiddling with objects such as pens, highlighters, etc.	
Other	

Now that you have completed these two tables, compare them to see how your mannerisms change from rest to presentation.

TOOLKIT EXERCISE 7

KNOWING WHEN TO STOP RESEARCHING YOUR TOPIC

In Chapter 9 of the book, we discussed how important it is to know when to stop researching your topic so that you do not end up over-researching and wasting time later on trying to cut this back. What follows is the template of a document that can help you collect sufficient detail for your speech.

The topic research template

When you need to research a new topic, take some time to determine some questions that your audience would want to see answered or discussed as part of your speech, as discussed in Chapter 8. Template 1 will give you some guidance as to the number of questions you should be looking for, as well as details to keep in mind while researching. Once you have determined these questions, use Template 2 for your research, using one page for each of your questions.

TEMPLATE 1

How long is your speech? (*Answer in minutes*)
The number of questions your should aim to address (*work out by taking length of speech ÷ 10*)
What is the focus of the conference?
What type of audience do you have?

TEMPLATE 2

Question number: (*Write out question*)
Source of information:
Details of information found:
1
2
3
4
5
6
7
8
9

In Template 2, you will see that you have been given space to enter details of nine sources of information. This is the maximum number of references you should research for any one question. It does not mean that you need to complete all the boxes, and you may find for some questions that you only have one reference. However, the point is that you never exceed nine for the purposes of researching a speech.

TEMPLATE FOR DEVELOPING YOUR SPEECH NOTES

What follows is a template for you to use to develop your speech notes, as discussed in Chapter 10. In the template, I have worked with four sections for your speech. Should you have fewer, leave these blank.

Section heading	Key points	Additional comments (e.g. points of emphasis, graphics, movement)
INTRODUCTION		
Section 1 (e.g. History of the subject)		
Section 2		

Section 3		
Section 4		
CONCLUSION		

175

Further Reading

Emotional Freedom Technique (EFT) or tapping

Beer, S. and Roberts, E. (2013) *Step-by-Step Tapping: EFT – The Amazing Self-help Technique to Heal Body and Mind*. London: Octopus Publishing Group.

Ortner, N. (2013) *The Tapping Solution: A Revolutionary System for Stress-Free Living*. London: Hay House.

Developing your speaking voice

Apps, J. (2012) *Voice and Speaking Skills for Dummies*. Chichester, West Sussex: John Wiley and Sons.

Despite the name, it is a good resource!

Fleming, C.A. (2013) *It's the Way You Say It: Becoming Articulate, Well-Spoken, and Clear*. Chichester, San Francisco: Berrett-Koehler.

References

American Psychiatric Publishing (2013) *Diagnostic and Statistical Manual of Mental Disorders, Fifth Edition (DSM-5)*. Arlington, VA: American Psychiatric Publishing.

Attwood, T. (2007) *The Complete Guide to Asperger's Syndrome*, London: Jessica Kingsley Publishers.

Bergemann, R. (2014) *An Asperger's Guide to Entrepreneurship*, London: Jessica Kingsley Publishers.

Collins Dictionaries (2013) *Collins Concise English Dictionary*. Glasgow: HarperCollins Publishers.

Grandin, T. (2006) *Thinking in Pictures*. London: Bloomsbury Publishing.

Murray, D., Lester, M. and Lawson, W. (2005) 'Asperger syndrome in forensic settings.' *International Journal of Forensic Mental Health 1*, 59–70.

Oxford University Press (2010) *Oxford Dictionary of English*. Oxford: Oxford University Press.

Index

CPSIA information can be obtained at www.ICGtesting.com
Printed in the USA
BVOW08s1608130415

395733BV00003B/7/P